100
Great Football Memories

from Norwich City Football Club's first 100 years

Edited by Peter Rogers

JARROLD
publishing

Contents

2002 4

5 **2002**

Acknowledgements

Norwich City Football Club and Jarrold Publishing would like to extend sincere thanks to everyone who has made this publication possible.

The credit for the idea of this book and its title lies at the feet of the Club's Director of Sales and Marketing, Andrew Cullen. Along with members of the Centenary working group, Andrew has also contributed to the publication and has shown great enthusiasm in seeing the original idea through to arriving on the bookshelves.

Finding those that are happy to talk about all things yellow and green is not a problem. However finding those that are then happy to put their thoughts and memories into words is not such an easy task, therefore we are indebted to all of our individual contributors.

In addition to those that have provided the written word I must also thank Club Secretary Kevan Platt for allowing access to his collection of programmes and Pink Uns, many of which are illustrated throughout the pages of this publication. We are again grateful to the Canary fans who granted permission for their photographs to be used in the publication of the Centenary Edition of Canary Citizens, a selection of those images have been used to enhance this book. Club photographer, Roger Harris has once again been of great assistance as have The Picture Library of Eastern Counties Newspapers Group Ltd.

I would like place on record my sincere thanks to Malcolm Crampton and the staff at Jarrold for their help and advice in seeing this project through to completion.

Finally I would like to say thank you to all of the players that have pulled on a Norwich City shirt throughout the Club's first 100 years and given so many memories to all that have followed the fortunes of the Canaries.

Peter Rogers
31 October 2002

Foreword

Having been fortunate enough to play 477 first team games for the Club I know just how difficult it is when someone asks me to name my favourite game or the most memorable moment from my playing days. Therefore I can imagine just how difficult it has been for the contributors to this book to make their choice of game.

My own entry reflects on my league debut against Tottenham Hotspur back in November 1986. Being my first league game it was special in its own right and the fact that one of my own boyhood heroes, Ray Clemence, was in goal for Tottenham only added to a memorable occasion. At the time of course I had no idea that it would be the first of 390 league games that I would go on to play for the Club.

Bryan celebrates victory in Munich, October 1993

During my career with Norwich City Football Club I have been privileged to work with some great players, managers and coaches. Of course players, managers and coaches come and go, the people who remain with the Club, season after season, are its supporters. The supporters here at Norwich City are in my mind second to none and the strong feelings and passions they have for the Club are demonstrated perfectly thoughout the pages of this publication.

Bryan Gunn
Sheriff of Norwich 2002
31 October 2002

Bryan in his current role as Sheriff of Norwich, June 2002

Jubilant crowd scenes following Norwich City's triumph in the FA Cup third round against Liverpool, 6 January 1951

Designed and produced by Jarrold Publishing
All photographs © Norwich City Football Club
Project Manager: Malcolm Crampton
Design: Kaarin Wall
Edited by Peter Rogers, Tom Albrighton and Sonya Calton
Managing Editor: Sarah Letts

Printed in Great Britain. Jarrold Publishing 1/02
www.jarrold-publishing.co.uk/specialpublishing

JARROLD
publishing

Introduction

All football fans know about the excitement generated by a goal, the relief felt at the final whistle of a 1-0 win and the heartbreak of defeat. Throughout the pages of this book, fans, managers and players of Norwich City Football Club describe their own memories from the Canaries' first 100 years.

There have of course been many highs and lows in the history of our great Club and obviously we all have our most memorable match and favourite player. You may well be surprised to see certain games not mentioned in this publication and equally you may wonder just why certain games have been chosen as someone's favourite. That is of course the beauty of football; the same match can be viewed in many different ways by many individual supporters.

We have been fortunate enough to obtain a recollection of the Canaries' former home, The Nest, as well as fans and players memories of the famous '58/'59 Cup run, arguably the event that put Norwich City on the footballing map. Many City supporters still cite promotion to the top flight in '71/'72 as their happiest time of following the Club and those never to be forgotten matches at Brisbane Road and Vicarage Road are described fondly over the coming pages.

Whatever gets the yellow and green blood in your veins racing, whether it be Wembley, promotion, Europe, Cardiff or a last minute winner at Portman Road, there is certainly something for you in this unique publication.

The first century of Norwich City Football Club has provided some fantastic memories for those that have been fortunate enough to see events unfold. And I have no doubt the next 100 years will follow in a similar fashion.

On the ball City!

Peter Rogers
November 2002

Adam Aiken • Terry Allcock • Geoffrey Belson • Keith Bertschin • Kathy Blake • Richard Bland • James Blower • Roy Blower • John Bond • Bobby Brennan • Mark Burchett • Mike Burt • Standley Bushell • Callum Butcher • Conor Butcher • Rob Butcher • Sharon Butcher • Geoff Butler • Ian Butterworth • Tony Chapman • Gary Cheeseman • Charles Clarke • Olly Cook • Tim Cook • Mark Cracknell • Andrew Cullen • Graeme Davies • John Deehan • Neil Doncaster • Martin Eagle • Rob Emery • Bryan W. Farmer • Sandra Fishwick • Duncan Forbes • Richard Futter • Angus George • Ian Gibson • Trevor Godbold • Susan Gorman • Robert Gray • Sarah Greaves • Bryan Gunn • Erica Halfhold-Nelson • Matt Hansell • Tony Harper • Ben Hawksley • Myra Hawtree • George Howard • Daniel Kinsman • John Landamore • David Machin • Dave Major • Jason Masala • John McNamara • Nicholas Mead • Peter Meades • Peter Mendham • Keith Newton • Shaun Otway • Russell Parker • Kevin Piper • Kevan Platt • Bill Punton • Malcolm Robertson • Peter Rogers • Glen Sandell • Lee Shepherd • Peter Silvester • Tim Skinner • Barry Skipper • Paul Slater • Delia Smith • Kelvin Smith • Steve Smith • Dave Stringer • Catherine Swallow • Oliver Sweetman • Martin Thirkettle • Simon Thomas • David Thornhill • Judy Trivett • Steve Trivett • David Tubby • Roy Waller • Mrs P. Watling • Keith Webb • James Woodrow

1

George Howard, whose scrapbook enabled his daughter Jill to recall this match from The Nest

I am writing this on behalf of my father, George Howard, who was the longest-serving employee of Norwich City Football Club, having worked in the lottery department and programme sales office for many years. I have read through his own memory book of The Nest and Carrow Road and have chosen this match.

Memories of the Nest

Norwich City 0–1 Sheffield Wednesday ⚽ FA Cup fifth round ⚽ 16 February 1935

By George Howard

Over 25,000 spectators attended this fifth-round tie at the Nest, which Sheffield Wednesday were said to be extremely lucky to have won. Only Jack Brown, their goalkeeper, saved them from being humiliated. In the first half he made two great saves from Russell and Burditt. Sam Bowen, full-back, was certainly on the ball that day, as was John Scott. He kept a firm hold in the middle and closely marked Wednesday's Palethorpe, who had little choice but to stay in the background for most of the game.

The City forwards were a stronger line than Wednesday's. They showed skill and pace but they could never quite hit that ball into the net. Russell outpaced the Wednesday backs and gave them no rest.

With no goals in sight, it was beginning to look like Norwich would have to travel to Sheffield for a replay, when all of a sudden cheers from Wednesday fans erupted. Palethorpe moved far from the right, was passed the ball from Hooper, and lobbed the ball over the City players in front of the goal. Rimmer gave it that final touch into the net. Norwich City were once again out of the FA Cup.

Man of the Match had to be Wednesday's goalkeeper, Brown, who saved everything that the Norwich team threw at him.

2

Now a resident of Eastbourne in Sussex, Brian has followed the Canaries for over 50 years. The first match he attended was a wartime fixture between Norwich City and the Royal Engineers.

Docherty's match

Norwich City 3–1 Liverpool ⚽ FA Cup third round ⚽ 6 January 1951

By Bryan W. Farmer

In over fifty years of following the Canaries there have been so many memorable moments to savour: in both victory and defeat, promotion and relegation, from Division Three (South) to the old First Division and on into the Premiership and Europe. Then there have been so many thrilling and ecstatic moments in the FA Cup, and the Wembley appearances in the League Cup and Milk Cup. With such a vast reservoir of memories, it's almost impossible to single out just one favourite moment. But there is one match at Carrow Road that confirmed me as a lifelong follower of Norwich, and a moment in that match when I lost my hat and my heart to the club. It is Norwich City–Liverpool in the third round of the FA Cup 1950/51 – the match that came to be known as 'Docherty's match'.

From the moment the draw was made I knew this game would be something special. Liverpool, beaten finalists the previous year, were expected to go one better this time. In my youth, I had spent many a holiday with my Geordie relations and so had seen the England and Liverpool centre-forward Albert Stubbins on many occasions in the black and white stripes of Newcastle United, his previous club, and been thrilled by his goal-scoring abilities. On the wing for the Reds was the inimitable Billy Liddell, an outstanding Scottish international. Liverpool, then as now, were true football giants, a First Division team bristling with international talent. Norwich were playing in the old Third Division (South) and, though they later gained something of a reputation for giant-killing in the FA Cup, they were still minnows in the football pond. But we knew that in Ron Ashman we had a courageous captain; in Ron Foulkes we had a rock of a centre-half; in Ken Nethercott we had a safe pair of hands; and in Gavin, Kinsey, Hollis and Eyre we had forwards who could play football and score goals.

We travelled over from King's Lynn on the train, got to the ground by twelve o'clock and were in the Barclay eating our sandwiches before half past. I believe the gate that day was in the region of 35,000, and by kick-off the excitement was intense. The teams came out to a wall of noise that seemed to go on for the full ninety minutes. I don't recall seeing any Liverpool supporters, though there must have been some, and though they are renowned for their singing nowadays, we sang 'On the ball, City' loudly enough to drown out loudspeaker announcements and couldn't hear even our neighbours speak! Every attack, every saving tackle, brought a new chorus of the anthem. Norwich were well and truly holding their own, hustling and harrying the Liverpool stars into errors that drew great roars from the terraces. I confess to feeling a little disappointed that Stubbins hadn't had a kick as Reg Foulkes marshalled his defence, Bill Lewis tackled like the thumper those who saw him will know he was, whilst Ashman and Pickwick in midfield were cutting out danger and feeding their hard-running forwards.

Somehow, early in the second half I think, the new boy from Lincoln City, Tom Docherty, put the finish on a loose ball in the area and, unbelievably, we were in the lead.

Tom Docherty who scored twice against Liverpool was back at Carrow Road for the Centenary reunion

Stung by this reverse, Liverpool came back at us, flinging all their talented resources into achieving an equaliser that would take us back to Anfield for a replay and almost certain defeat. Wave after wave of red shirts bore down on the Barclay End like a red tide, only to be thwarted by indomitable defenders playing well beyond their normal energy and skill levels, urged on by the roaring throng behind them. When it seemed that all was lost and Liverpool must score, there was Ken Nethercott clawing the ball out of the air above Stubbins' red hair or diving to right and left to punch or catch that brown leather ball to his vivid green jersey. What a player, what a match – could we hold on?

In the 75th minute City went two up through Eyre. With about ten minutes to go City worked the ball out of defence and across to Docherty who squirmed past one defender and avoided a lunging tackle from another. As Crossley, Liverpool's Welsh international goalkeeper, advanced, our man unleashed an unstoppable shot with his lethal left foot and the ball finished in the corner of the River End goal.

Carrow Road erupted! As we celebrated in that cauldron of noise and emotion, someone grabbed my hat and threw it heavenward. I never saw it again, but I didn't care. What a moment, what a goal, what a team, what a result! Norwich City became my team at that never-to-be-repeated moment. In my mind's eye I can see it still, through the murk of a winter's afternoon, the ball nestling in the net, the downcast Liverpool team collapsing to the ground in despair as the Canaries jumped for joy and the Barclay echoed to the rafters with the now-famous anthem… 'On the ball, City!'

3

My favourite match

Norwich City 3–1 Liverpool ☾ FA Cup third round ☾ 6 January 1951

By Barry Skipper CBE

Barry Skipper is a Company Director and Vice Chairman of Norwich City Football Club. He attended his first Canaries match on 17 May 1947 – a home fixture against Walsall which the Saddlers won 2–0.

At the age of twelve, five foot one and six stone ten pounds in the depth of a pre-central heating winter, Saturday's football match was always the highlight of my week. Especially when it was back to school the following Wednesday after the Christmas and new year break. This particular new year was especially exciting, as City were in the third round of the FA Cup, with a home draw. Not that you really understand the entire significance of the Cup at twelve. Somewhere down the road, in May, two teams against whom Norwich never

Barry was in the crowd (bottom right) for the FA Cup win over Liverpool on 6 January 1951

played would fill the back pages of the newspapers and be gabbled about on the radio all day, before we schoolboys turned our minds to cricket, athletics and the summer to come.

With Saturday's Cup tie looming, the most urgent consideration was the weather. Wintry showers had persisted all week and it was not so much a question of whether the pitch would be OK, but whether Dad would risk the Hillman on a trip from Diss to Norwich if there was the prospect of an icy drive back in the dark.

The Saturday football ritual was always the same. My mother and seven-year-old sister Julia came too, and this could be dodgy, since Julia had a propensity to be car sick, usually just through Newton Flotman. They didn't come to the match; they visited Gran and Grandad, who lived in Florence Road, Thorpe Hamlet. Grandad always reserved a parking space for father with a metal bucket painted yellow and green.

Grandad had been an avid City fan when they played at the Nest, which was only a few hundred yards from Florence Road. Before matches he would earn his admission by storing spectators' bikes in his little front garden, securing them to the iron railings. The railings were subsequently removed during the Second World War to be made into guns – or so they said. With the move to Carrow Road, the bike-storing business moved to the 'new' ground. Dad had a season ticket, so he went to Gran's for lunch, although I think they called it dinner.

I got dropped off at the ground around noon, so I could secure a spot on the front rails for a 1.45pm January kick-off. As yet we had no floodlights – it would be some time before Len Shackleton and Sunderland would come to open them. This particular match marked the debut of two of my Christmas presents: a rosette my Gran had made me and a cleaned-up rattle, which I suspect had seen its best days at the Nest.

I always went to matches alone, but when I got to the front rail, all my football friends were there. The same faces came week in and week out, and a wonderful camaraderie developed. None of us knew one another's names, nor where we lived, neither did we care. The only clues were the badges on the various school caps we inevitably wore. Mine said Initium Sapientiae Timor Domini – an instant giveaway that I went to Diss Grammar School. Who minded – we were all linked in the fervour of cheering on the Canaries, win, lose or draw.

Once the turnstiles opened it was a rush to the rails, to get as close to the centre circle as you could. My spot was the open terrace opposite where the players came out. Little did I know it would one day be covered, all-seater, and glory in the name of the South Stand. This particular Saturday I got about twenty yards from the penalty box at the Barclay End, and clearly it was going to be a big crowd. The hour or so before the game flashed by as we all soaked up the atmosphere, late-coming schoolboys being passed overhead by the men in flat caps behind us.

Then, just before the players ran out, we had a great treat. The photographer from the Pink Un appeared in front of us and invited a cheer and a wave, which we duly gave. I suspect that with us up against First Division opposition, he didn't think we would have much to shout about later. I always felt sorry for that photographer. Two quick pictures, one at each end, then off he would traipse down the tunnel to ensure the Pink Un had a photo for the front page of the paper, which would be on the streets by 5pm.

In the first half City attacked the Barclay End. These were the days of inside-rights and left halves. Our number eight was my favourite; not very tall, he always opened his mouth as he headed the ball, a technique I had sought to perfect on my debut for the Grecians versus the Persians in a house match last term, but with limited success.

The great thing about being squeezed on the rails only a foot or so from the pitch is you get to hear all the chat and shouting between the players. On my school report for the previous term, PT master Reggie Wright had had the audacity to say, 'quite good, but has a tendency to shout too much during the game'. That's how much he knew about real football! The next term I had another 'tendency', this time it was 'to argue with the referee's decision'. Now in his seventies and President of the Old Dysseans Association, I hope Reggie has finally realised just how ahead of my time I was!

The other thing about being squashed at the front aged twelve is that the best recollections you have of the game are the incidents that happen closest to you. After a goalless first half, my number eight hero laid the ball to our number eleven, who smashed it into the net. What an eruption! Within minutes we scored again, our number ten volleying a left-foot shot from the edge of the box. The noise was simply unbelievable – two-nil up.

With fifteen minutes to go, the opposition turned up the heat, their star studded internationals' reputations at risk. Their number six was particularly aggressive and switched to the right-hand side of the pitch (my side). Suddenly he was forging forward, nearly level with me with what seemed little between

1951

him and the goal. Then, out of the gathering murk, a yellow flash of blonde hair appeared, along with a sliding tackle that seemed to have started at Thorpe Station. It took ball, number six, and all, and both players crashed into the railings right in front of me. What I now know as a profanity came from the mouth of the dispossessed manager – six championships, three League Cups, one UEFA Cup, one Euro Super Cup and three European Cups to his name. Our number three got up and ruffled my school cap – yes, Bill Lewis actually touched me. We scored again, then they scored in the last minute, but nothing mattered, for the rest of the game, the next day, and the weekend – indeed for the whole of January. Bill Lewis had touched me!

Back at Gran's, everyone was very pleased, even my sister who really just wanted to listen to the Ovalteenies. Well everyone except Gran – she was upset the Government had just reduced the meat ration by 2d per person per week, apparently due to continuing difficulties with Argentina. Why do the Argies always spoil everything to do with football?

4

Beating the Gunners

Arsenal 1–2 Norwich City ⚽ FA Cup fourth round ⚽ 30 January 1954

by Myra Hawtree

Myra's love of football continues on into her retirement and in 2002 she attended the World Cup in Japan.

My favourite memory is of my first-ever away match, at Highbury in the FA Cup on 30 January 1954, when City beat Arsenal two-one in front of a crowd of 55,767.

I went to the match by train with my dad, a lifelong City supporter. It was a very cold, snowy day. I remember standing at the match very low down in a front enclosure and my dad giving me some newspaper to stand on to try to keep my feet warm.

City went one-nil down in the game, missed a penalty and then had Bobby Brennan (my favourite player) sent off, together with Alex Forbes of Arsenal, after

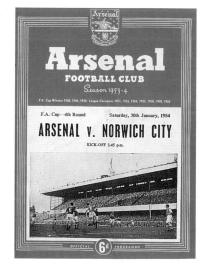

The programme from the Canaries' FA Cup triumph at Highbury

they got into a bit of a fight. City fought back and Tommy Johnston scored two goals to win us the game. I recall that near the end of the game our goalie, Ken Oxford, made a great save and landed on his head – we all thought he must have broken his neck but luckily he hadn't.

Norwich received a lot of coverage in the national press before and after the game, as we were only in Division Three (South) at the time. My lasting memory is the image of Bill Lewis consoling Arthur Milton of Arsenal at the end of the game. Arthur Milton was also a county cricketer with Gloucestershire at the time.

5

Hooked on Norwich

Norwich City 1–2 Leicester City ⚽ FA Cup fifth round ⚽ 20 February 1954

By Mrs P. Watling

In her account Mrs Watling describes the excitement of her first ever match at Carrow Road. Nearly 50 years on she is still a keen follower of the Canaries.

The Pink Un following City's cup exit at the hands of Leicester City

Although I was born in August 1933, I suppose you could say that I went to my first match some time late in 1932! My Mum was expecting me, and she and my dad went to the Nest at that time.

However, I actually went to my first match on 20 February 1954. It was the fifth round of the FA Cup against Leicester City. We led one-nil at half-time, but lost two-one. I believe it was a horrible day, and we stood at the River End huddled under waterproofs. I had just started a new job, and was asked if I would like to join the office, as they were all going to the match. I went, and after that game I was hooked!

Eastern Football News
(THE PINK UN)
NORWICH, SATURDAY, FEBRUARY 20, 1954

CUP SPECIAL

Price 2d.

SPORTS TROUSERS
IN LOVAT WORSTED
30 in. to 38 in. Waist
63/-
Bonds
ALL SAINTS GREEN, NORWICH. Tel. 23166

'HIGHBURY' THIS TIME

Two in three minutes turn the tide

AFTER BRENNAN GOAL

NORWICH CITY 1   LEICESTER CITY 2

FOR the third time in their history Norwich City have failed in the fifth round of the F.A. Cup. At Carrow Road today before a 40,000 crowd (receipts £5693) they

LATE NEWS
FOOTBALL RESULTS
Torquay 2, Bournemouth 0.
Buckie 7, Peebles 2.
Fulham 5, Luton 1.
Bristol ...

1954

A young supporter

Norwich City 3–0 Manchester United ◐ FA Cup third round ◐ 10 January 1959

By James Woodrow

Like many other fans, James' favourite match was the very first one he attended during Norwich's 1959 FA Cup run.

Signatures from the programme from the famous victory over the Busby Babes in 1959

I remember nothing of this game. I was four and a half years old and had not yet become entwined with the club. I know now that we met Manchester United in the third round of the Cup at Carrow Road – my first match. I know that we outplayed them in the snow, hit the bar, hit the post, and won three-nil. I know what followed; that despite being a Third Division team we nearly got to Wembley. I know that my father had thought that one day I'd be proud to be able to say 'I was there'. He was, as I admit has sometimes been the case, right.

A classic in the snow

Norwich City 3–0 Manchester United ◐ FA Cup third round ◐ 10 January 1959

By David Tubby

David Tubby attended his first match at Carrow Road on 17 March 1956, when Norwich beat QPR 1–0.

Searching through my childhood scrapbooks, it was a non-Canary cutting that first caught my attention. 'The £45,000 soccer player' was the sports headline of the Daily Express in September 1958. Manchester United's Matt Busby, as part of his rebuilding exercise following the devastating Munich air crash, had signed Albert Quixall from Sheffield Wednesday for a record British transfer fee. Quixall joined Bobby Charlton and Dennis Violett to form a potent United attacking spearhead, and a little under four months later he and his famous colleagues were to play a part in Norwich City's most famous run in the FA Cup.

Forty-three years ago, on Saturday 10 January 1959, I had spent the morning persuading my dad that the snow was not deep enough to stop us driving from Caister to see the match. Snow and dodgy driving conditions were the least of thirteen-year-olds' concerns – I wanted to see the mighty Manchester United, and held out little hope of a City victory.

Over the years my memories of this day have obviously dimmed, but I can still remember my red and black hooped school football socks being warmed in front of the fire, pulling them on and bending the tops over the top of my wellies. I hadn't appreciated that United too would be wearing red and black socks that day.

I remember climbing into our old light grey Standard Ten Companion, and as we crawled out of Caister we skidded sharply. I saw the concern on dad's face and prayed he wouldn't turn back. He didn't. We picked up my granddad in Fleggburgh and arrived safely in Norwich – in those days we usually parked in either Cedar Road or Harbour Road. Looking at the width of these roads today, it doesn't seem possible.

The match must have been all-ticket, as I still have the left-hand torn half in my scrapbook, with 'Price 2/-' printed in the left-hand corner. Having handed over our tickets we managed to find a space fairly near the rails fronting the pitch, roughly where the away support sits today. The crowd was supposed to be 38,000, but I don't seem to recall it as being so tightly packed as for the Tottenham replay. Perhaps the snow did deter some ticket holders from turning up – if so, they missed a classic!

My memories of the match are vague. Possibly because of our position on the terracing, I can recall visions of both right wingers: our own speedy Errol Crosan flying on the snow, and United's Warren Bradley, who did not impress and was excellently marked by Ron Ashman. We must have been about level with the penalty area, as I can recall the elation at seeing Terry Bly's first goal thunder into the net at the Barclay End. It warmed the crowd on a bitterly cold day, a day when fans had to stamp their feet on the terracing to relieve tingling toes. I have a wonderful newspaper photograph of Harry Gregg holding on to the Crossan header – did it cross the line?

I remember the teams' strips: red shirts with white shorts and yellow shirts with black shorts against a background of snow. I watched in awe at the sure-footedness of those yellow-shirted heroes, and wondered why United's players were so tentative. It was not until some time later that Archie Macaulay's tactic of cutting away part of the studs to reveal the nails for better grip was revealed.

I still have the half-ticket, programme, Eastern Daily Press report and the pre- and post-match Pink Uns. What a pity very little, if any, of that match is preserved on film.

Terry Allcock shoots for goal against Manchester United

Oh, and what of Albert Quixall and his famous partners? The Eastern Daily Press reported that 'Charlton was but the palest of shadows of his great self, while it was necessary to take an occasional peep at the programme to make sure it was the £45,000 Quixall at inside right – so completely was he overshadowed by the City defence.'

8

No need for Ninian

Norwich City 3–2 Cardiff City ⚽ FA Cup fourth round ⚽ 24 January 1959

By Roy Blower

Roy Blower is known to most Canary fans in his role as Chairman of the Norwich City Independent Supporters Association.

Life-long City fan Roy Blower had no hesitation in naming the fourth game in the famous 1958/59 Cup run as his favourite City match

My first recollection of Norwich City is as a five-year-old in 1948, when I saw Terry Ryder playing for the reserves. For the last forty-five years I have missed just a handful of games, so have plenty of matches to choose from for the most memorable. The one that stands out in my memory is the FA Cup fourth round tie between Norwich City and Cardiff City played at Carrow Road on 24 January 1959.

The excitement and crowd involvement of the whole occasion was tremendous, but it is the late drama that elevates this game to the top of my list. I can remember Bonson equalising for Cardiff with about twenty minutes to go, and as Ken Nethercott picked the ball out of the net I think everyone thought we were off to Ninian Park for a replay.

The game seemed to be wending its way to its expected conclusion when Terry Bly changed the course of events. Errol Crossan worked the ball to Bly, who was in a wide left position. Bly then blasted a shot past the goalkeeper from an unbelievably narrow angle. I can picture it now – it went in like an arrow, definitely one of the best goals ever seen at Carrow Road.

This match is generally remembered as the hardest game in City's memorable 1958/59 FA Cup run which took them to the semi-final stage where they were finally eliminated by Luton Town in a replay.

Although Cardiff were only a Second Division team, they were still a very good side. It was after this game that the people of Norfolk began to believe that the team were going places and that we were 'on a roll'. It was a fantastic time for all City fans.

Thanks Ken

Sheffield United 1–1 Norwich City ⚽ FA Cup sixth round ⚽ 28 February 1959

By Bobby Brennan

The late Bobby Brennan played 250 games for the Canaries and scored fifty-two goals during two spells at the Club, the first between 1953–56 and the second more successful period, between 1957–60. An extremely gifted inside forward, he won five caps for Northern Ireland and played for Luton, Birmingham and Fulham before joining City in July 1953 for £15,000, a then-record fee.

My most memorable game is the famous FA Cup run of 1958/59. On 28 February 1959 the Canaries travelled to Bramall Lane to face First Division Sheffield United in front of 57,000 spectators.

It was a marvellous occasion and a tremendous match. Sheffield United felt that this was their year to win the Cup. After they scored early on they must have been very confident – their confidence increasing when City goalkeeper Ken Nethercott injured his shoulder badly midway through the first half. Ken was a great man and to his credit he bravely completed the remainder of the game.

I was more relieved than anyone when he continued, as I was due to go in goal if he went off. I didn't want to, of course, but no one else fancied it. I had done a bit of goalkeeping in training, but keeping goal in an FA Cup quarter-final would have been totally different. My only previous experience had been when I went in goal for Fulham at Leicester when our goalkeeper Ian Black was injured. We lost six-nil then, so you can understand why I wasn't keen to replace Ken!

Surprisingly, we took heart from Ken's injury and virtually outplayed Sheffield United for the rest of the game. An Errol Crossan 'goal' was disallowed, before Bobby played his part in a seventy-fifth-minute equaliser. I beat a couple of players to lay a chance for Errol to score.

It was a great achievement to hold them. I can remember how strange it was playing in a stadium with only three sides, as Bramall Lane was still used for cricket in those days.

I can recall later games in the Cup run too. I scored an early goal in the replay against Sheffield United in our three-two win. In the semi-final against my old club, Luton, at White Hart Lane, I am convinced we should have won the game. I was dreading having to play against Luton. I would much have preferred Nottingham Forest. As it was, in the first

Bobby sends in a powerful shot during the cup tie at Bramall Lane

game we had another 'goal' disallowed before I equalised to earn us a replay.

It was my thirty-fourth birthday that day, but a Cup Final place was not to be, as Luton won the replay at St Andrews one-nil.

They were great times, we had a superb bunch of lads and I well remember the sense of fun involved in going out each Saturday to do something you enjoyed. Although I haven't been to Carrow Road for thirty-odd years now, I know football isn't the same any more – it's very serious now, with all the big money around.

10

Cup glory

Norwich City 3–2 Sheffield United ☾ FA Cup sixth round replay ☾ 4 March 1959

By Terry Allcock

Terry Allcock played for the Canaries between March 1958 and April 1969, during which time he played 389 senior games and scored 127 goals. A powerful forward, he switched to a much more defensive role later in his Carrow Road career, a move that prevented him from overhauling Johnny Gavin's club record of 132 senior goals.

With nearly 400 games to choose from it is not surprising that I found it difficult to single out one match as the most memorable.

I have lots of good memories from my career, but I guess the famous FA Cup run of 1958/59 stands out above all the others. All of the games in that run are still very vivid for me, but if I had to single out one game it would be the sixth-round replay against Sheffield United at Carrow Road, played on 4 March 1959.

The intensity of the crowd was fantastic, it was a real emotional occasion and the singing before the match was unbelievable. Once the game started all you could hear was the volume, but they helped us to a great three-two win.

Bobby Brennan and Terry Bly had put the Canaries two-nil up inside thirty-two minutes before Pace pulled one back before half-time following an error by debutant goalkeeper Sandy Kennon. Bly made it three-one before a late goal from Summers sent a few Canary hearts thumping in the closing minutes.

It was an outstanding achievement to reach the semi-final of the FA Cup and that season was a launchpad to promotion the following season.

The programme from the FA Cup replay with the Blades at Carrow Road

Replay on the radio

Norwich City 0–1 Luton ☻ FA Cup Replay ☻ 18 March 1959

By Trevor Godbold

Trevor Godbold got the Canary habit at a young age, attending his first match at age seven in 1958. On that occasion the Canaries were at home to Accrington Stanley but lost the match 3–0.

It might seem strange that my most memorable game involving the Canaries resulted in defeat, and perhaps even stranger that I didn't even attend the match!

The date was 18 March, 1959. I was a small boy of seven, and as the match was played on a Wednesday afternoon, I was actually at school that day. In those days every lad who was interested in football followed his local team – no southern Manchester United or Liverpool supporters then. I can recall one lad who joined our school after moving down from Huddersfield; it was really strange to meet someone who had an interest in another football team.

I had followed the Canaries' Cup progress through my father, who was a long-time City fan. He had told me stories about the speed of 'Cowboy Crossan' and the goal-scoring exploits of Terry Bly.

The FA Cup seemed so much more exciting years ago. All the boys would listen to the Cup draw on the wireless at Monday lunchtime, hoping for a home tie against a famous First Division side.

The Canaries were in the old Third Division and had beaten the likes of Manchester United and Tottenham Hotspur to get to the semi-final. This game was a replay, arranged after a one-all draw with Luton Town at White Hart Lane on the preceding Saturday.

On the afternoon of the replay the headmaster of St Faith's Primary School, Mr Bourke, stopped our games lesson early and told us all to follow him into the school hall. The whole school assembled in the hall to listen to the wireless commentary live from St Andrew's, Birmingham. I still remember that the commentary often seemed to be somewhat behind the action, judging by the sound of the crowd reactions that could be heard from the wireless.

We all listened and hoped for a Norwich victory. I can still recall the moment when the goal was scored. We heard a roar and all assumed it was a Canary goal – how we jumped and shouted, until we were informed that it was actually Billy Bingham of Luton who had scored. That minute, which I now know was the fifty-sixth, was to be a minute that brought heartache to thousands of Norwich City supporters and to one seven-year-old boy who has never quite recovered from it.

I remember how we were all told to make our way home before the end of the game. School finished on time in those days! I rushed home in the hope of

The programme from the Canaries' one and only appearance in an FA Cup semi-final replay

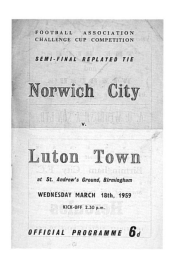

FOOTBALL ASSOCIATION
CHALLENGE CUP COMPETITION

SEMI-FINAL REPLAYED TIE

Norwich City

v.

Luton Town

at St. Andrew's Ground, Birmingham

WEDNESDAY MARCH 18th, 1959

KICK-OFF 2.30 p.m.

OFFICIAL PROGRAMME 6d

getting to the wireless and hearing of an equaliser. I managed to hear the last few minutes, but unfortunately we didn't get that equaliser. Norwich were out of the Cup and I cried.

My dad had been at work – he wasn't allowed to take time off, even for a semi-final replay – and I was still upset when he arrived home. He must have been bitterly disappointed too, but he tried to cheer me up and promised to take me to a game for the first time. He did, later in the year; we beat Accrington Stanley four-one and I loved it.

I have been a regular supporter since 1961, but it is the Luton game that I will always remember as the match that broke my heart but tied me to Norwich City for life. To this day I still hate Luton Town and Billy Bingham, but I did find my first love, Norwich City Football Club. Despite all the ups and the many downs you can never get over your first love. Real supporters don't desert their team, even when faced with defeat and relegation. Tell that to the kids today!

12

Respect

Norwich City 4–3 Southend United ● Third Division ● 27 April 1960

By Bill Punton

Throughout his six-year career with Norwich City, Bill delighted the Carrow Road crowd with his fast and direct play. Now a pundit on local radio, Bill is a familiar sight at home fixtures.

In the 1959/60 season, City clinched promotion to Division Two with a four-three home win against my previous club, Southend. I scored one of the goals in the game, and it was something of a turning point in my Carrow Road career. For the first time, I felt that the fans respected me. I had replaced one of their great favourites, Bobby Brennan, and this goal endeared me to the fans.

It was vital for the team to achieve promotion that season, having enjoyed the FA Cup run the season before. If success had not been forthcoming, the team might have been broken up.

Bill Punton in his playing days

1960

13

Six against Stoke

Norwich 6–0 Stoke City ⚽ Second Division ⚽ 9 March 1963

By Kelvin Smith

Life-long Canaries fan, Kelvin Smith looks back on a time when City had real 'six appeal' a Jim Oliver hat-trick saw them crush Stoke City 6-0 at Carrow Road in March 1963.

I have been watching City since 1958, my first game being a floodlit friendly against West Ham United (we lost four-two to the First Division side). The first game is always significant, but for the best memory I would have to go for this game against Stoke City.

As we stood waiting for the kick-off, some changes to the City side were announced: Bill Punton, Tommy Bryceland and Jimmy Hill (arguably three of the finest players to wear the Norwich shirt after the Second World War) were out through injury. In their places came Jim Conway, Jim Oliver and Alistair Miller. The Stoke side included Stanley Matthews, Jackie Mudie and Denis Violett, and they were giving a debut to a new signing, Jimmy McIlroy. All of them were international players at one time or another. 'What chance have we got against that lot,' we thought!

However, in a five-minute spell in the first half City went three-nil up, through two goals by Oliver and one by Gerry Mannion. Even with this score at half-time, we were convinced it couldn't last. But it got better. Terry Allcock was going through a purple patch that season, and it was he who scored the fourth, smacking in a Mannion centre halfway through the second half. There was an added bonus to this goal – it was Allcock's 100th for the club. I can remember the crowd (at least in the South Stand where I was) going noisily berserk. Oliver made it five a little later, and in the last minute Jim Conway got in on the act by firing the sixth. We couldn't believe it! Six-nil against a side like that!

It turned out to be quite a week. The following Wednesday, City beat Newcastle five-nil in the FA Cup fourth round, two of those goals coming (I believe) in the first five minutes and Allcock scoring four. In fact that was the season that City's record crowd of nearly 44,000 turned up for the sixth round match against Leicester City (which we lost two-nil). I remember hundreds of people (of which I was one) on the track round the pitch, because there was no room on the terraces; Carrow Road was like a huge bowl of people that day. We only finished halfway up Division Two, but it was quite a year!

14

Speed triumphs over experience

Norwich City 6–0 Stoke City ☾ Second Division ☾ 9 March 1963

By Martin Eagle

Martin, a retired Sub Postmaster, was a regular on the Carrow Road stands in the early 1950s and remembers watching matches with his father. The first match he can remember distinctly was the Canaries' 5–1 victory over Port Vale on 12 September 1959.

The winter of 1962/63 was known as the 'big freeze' and caused most matches to be called off. Norwich's FA Cup third-round tie with Blackpool at Carrow Road was postponed eleven times, and the resulting fixture pile-up meant that the fifth-round draw read 'Walsall or Manchester City or Birmingham or Bury v. Norwich or Blackpool or Bradford City or Newcastle'!

Stoke City's visit was only the Canaries' third home game since December 29. Consequently, March 1963 was, probably, the busiest month in the club's history. Nine games were played – six won, one drawn and only two lost, twenty-three goals scored and fourteen conceded, including seven at Sunderland. Two notable away FA Cup victories were achieved; three-one at Blackpool and two-one at Manchester City. The month ended with the home sixth-round FA Cup match with Leicester City drawing a record attendance of 43,984.

I was only eleven in 1963, and football was still magical for me. It took the 1972 fog-abandoned League Cup semi-final with Chelsea to make me realise that Bill Shankly's famous quote – 'football is not just a matter of life and death, it's much more important than that' – was slightly wide of the mark. Journeying home over the bridge, although bitterly disappointed, the realisation came that at least we lived to fight again, and that there were more important things in life. The innocence of youth had evaporated.

But it was full of optimism and excitement that I left home on that rainy March Saturday – rattle in hand, bobble-hat on head, yellow and green scarf wrapped round my neck. This scarf was previously my father's, and had served him well during the 1958/59 cup run, but now it was customised with the sewn-on names of my heroes – Kelly, Bryceland, Mannion and Mullett – and those small star-shaped portrait badges that were sold outside the ground pinned on. In my pocket was the two shillings for the admission and fourpence for the programme, which quaintly described

GREENS SALE
LAST WEEK
Men's and Boys' wear
Final reductions
44 ST. BENEDICT'S

EASTERN
FOOTBAL
(THE PINK
No. 1378—Threepence

Jim Oliver, recalled to Hill, hits two

SIX-GUN

Canaries have the Potters' stars in a real whirl

NORWICH CITY 6   STOKE CITY 0
STOKE CITY'S big-name team were put on the rack at Carrow Road this afternoon.   At the end of it Matthews, McIlroy and Co. felt the heat licked to a frazzle by a Norwich City side who played the stuff the fans' dreams are made of.

Norwich as playing in 'black knickers'…

At two o'clock I was in place at the front of the River End. This was in the days of standing, with crash barriers spaced out on the terraces. Only a quarter of the ground was allocated for seating, and the River End was still open to the elements. If you stood there you could always walk around to other sections of the ground. Even if you weren't prepared to pay for the transfer, the gate that adjoined the South Stand, near the old half-time scoreboard, was opened during the second half.

Stoke City were chasing promotion. They were fifth in the League, six points behind the leaders Chelsea, but with three games in hand. Norwich were seventh, two points further adrift, having played the same number of matches as Chelsea. The Potters were a star-studded side, with Jimmy McIlroy, the current Irish international, signed from Burnley for £25,000 just days before the game. He joined three other internationals, Mudie (Scotland), Munich air-crash survivor Viollet (England) and the immortal Stanley Matthews (England) in a forward line boasting 154 international caps between them. Three other internationals lined up in defence: O'Neill (Eire), Allen (England) and Clamp (England).

Norwich had their own evergreen in acting player-manager Ron Ashman, a youthful thirty-six. He, Kennon and Allcock were the only survivors from the 1959 FA Cup semi-final. Of the others, Kelly, Staton, Oliver and Miller joined in the summer during the brief reign of manager George Swindin. Injury ruled out three of the Canaries' first-choice forward line – Conway came in for Bryceland and Oliver and Miller replaced Hill and Punton as the left-wing pair.

Ashman lost the toss and City kicked off towards the River End. All the opening pressure was from Norwich, with both Conway and Burton shooting narrowly wide. Stoke countered and Ratcliffe cut inside, his attempt skimming past the post. City won the first corner in the sixteenth minute from which Conway's cleared header resulted in another corner.

The match was settled with three goals in five minutes. Jim Oliver, put through the middle by a Conway pass, angled the ball past the goalkeeper to open the scoring in the thirteenth minute. O'Neill made a brilliant save from an Allcock header a minute later, but this only delayed the second goal. In the fifteenth minute Miller beat his man and turned the ball inside for Oliver to hammer home a left-foot drive from the edge of the penalty area. Three minutes later, Burton charged down O'Neill's clearance and the ball ran to Mannion, who nutmegged Allen and side-footed the ball between keeper and upright.

Stoke were now coming more into the game but were still second-best.

The Pink Un salutes six-goal City

'For Health and Comfort wear
AERTEX K.P.C. UNDERWEAR
Singlets and Briefs 7'6
Trunks 9'6

Bonds Man's Shop

n place of injured
utes…

CITY!

Norwich, although they had slackened their fierce pace, still looked dangerous in raids. Chances were being made and missed, with Conway and Allcock the culprits.

Stoke started the second half with purpose, with City content to let things stay as they were. Norwich received a wake-up call when Viollet, with only Kennon to beat, saw his shot saved. In the sixty-fifth minute 'the Count' (Terry Allcock) made it four with his 100th goal for the club. Mannion pulled the ball back and Allcock hammered it home. Oliver completed his hat-trick in the seventy-seventh minute with a precision header from a Mannion corner. Stoke rallied again, and McIlroy had a drive turned on to the bar by Kennon. In the final minute the crew-cut Scot, Conway, completed the rout, Mannion again the provider.

Norwich outwitted and outfought Stoke with the plan to use speed to counter the visitors' experience. Their slick, energetic attacking football tore the opposition's leaden-footed defence to pieces. This confidence and determination carried forward to midweek, and Newcastle were knocked out of the fourth round of the FA Cup five-nil. Surprisingly, the team was changed for this match, with Oliver, Saturday's hero, along with Conway and Miller, being replaced by Bryceland, Hill and Punton.

On returning home, the day was completed with the news that West Bromwich Albion had thrashed Ipswich six-one.

15

Playing truant

Norwich City 0–2 Leicester City ☾ FA Cup ☾ 30 March 1963

By Bryan W. Farmer

This is Brian's second great Norwich footballing moment.

Memories come thick and fast, and time lends enchantment to them. The 1959 cup run with that wonderful team led by the one and only Ron Ashman, promotion to the Second Division the following year, promotion to the First Division in 1972 led by Duncan Forbes, those halcyon days of the Premier League, and the unbelievably triumphant march into Europe. But Norwich City had always been formidable competitors in the FA Cup through the years, with wonderful performances over the whole of the first 100 years against clubs from the higher divisions. I witnessed many of these occasions, but one stands out in my memory, and strangely enough it was a day when my Canary team lost.

I was in my thirties at the time, married with a young family. The only way to progress in my line of work was to study for a professional qualification, and I was studying in the evenings at the West Norfolk Technical College in my home town. When examinations loomed, it was customary to have a day of revision work, organised by the professional body setting the exam. Though not compulsory, one was expected to take it seriously, so I and Sid, another student, signed up.

As the football season neared its end, we were delighted that our beloved Canaries were beating the likes of Newcastle and Manchester City in the FA Cup. But we were considerably dismayed to find that Norwich City were drawn at home to Leicester City in the quarter-finals on our study day. Like the sensible young men we were, we reasoned that we could see the Canaries any time and that we couldn't afford to miss the study day, especially as our employers subsidised our expenses. Our future prospects were far more important than a mere football match!

The local and national newspapers were, as always, full of the forthcoming match, which had really caught the imagination, and the match was a sell-out. On the day of the game, all roads in Norfolk led to Carrow Road… except ours. We motored through villages bedecked with yellow and green en route for the college. We arrived in good time and dutifully made our way to the appointed room, where an austere gentleman bade us sit down, along with twenty or thirty others, to start the day's work. Football forgotten, we worked quietly and studiously until the bell rang for lunchtime, when we decided to find a pub or a fish and chip shop, and made for the city centre. One house, or pub perhaps, had a loudspeaker outside relaying the strains of 'On the ball, City' to passers-by, the Canary anthem echoing in the narrow street. As we approached the castle, the Steward and Patterson dray, with its four beautifully turned-out horses and driver in top hat, clattered along the street all decorated in yellow and green. What a wonderful sight! It made the hairs stand up on the back of our necks in anticipation.

We looked at one another, but shook our heads. 'No, our destiny today is not at the match,' was the unspoken message that passed in the knowing looks we exchanged. Into the pub for a beer and a ham roll we went. It was around one o'clock and the pub was full of ruddy-faced men all talking animatedly about this afternoon's main event. Bets were being exchanged on the result, and good-natured banter about members of the Norwich team raised expectations of another memorable victory for the Canary underdogs.

1963

We finished our refreshment and were about to leave, feeling a bit out of place in our business suits among the fans up from the county in their yellow and green. As we headed for the door a fellow about our own age said to me, 'Know anyone want a couple of tickets bor?' I hesitated. 'My mates had to work today and couldn't come, anyone can have them for the price they paid, they just want their money back, that's all.' My heart skipped two beats. 'Hey, did you hear what he said?' Turning to Sid, I said, 'he wants to sell two tickets for the match! What do you say?' He pushed on by me, saying gloomily, 'you know we can't go. We've got to get back to the college.' 'Come on,' I replied, 'some people would give their right arm for a chance like this.'

Outside the pub, we stood and argued for a few moments. Sid was visibly weakening. Finally he said, 'Well, I guess we have worked hard this morning, they probably won't miss us if we don't go back, and it's only economics this afternoon, and after that beer I'll probably go to sleep... do you think he's sold them tickets yet?' We went back and sought out the chap with the tickets, who willingly parted with them – two standing at the River End.

'The study day doesn't end until five, so we will be back just as they are all leaving, and home at the right time too,' Sid said, 'so it will be OK.' With that we made our way down the Prince of Wales Road and along the river with the thousands pouring out of the station and from coaches in noisy anticipation of the big game. Caught up in the excitement of the moment, we began to discuss the chances of another semi-final appearance for our heroes, having both been to most of the 1959 cup run games. As was usual in those days, people arrived early to get a good place to stand, and we duly got into the ground around two o'clock, only to find it pretty well filled already.

As always on the big occasions, the atmosphere was electric, and when the lads came out the roar would have taken the roof off – had there been one in 1963. Of the match itself I remember very little, except for one incident. Leicester

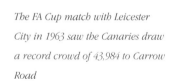

No 725
NORWICH CITY FOOTBALL CLUB
F.A. CUP SEMI-FINALISTS, SEASON 1958-59
FOOTBALL LEAGUE CUP WINNERS, SEASON 1961-62

F.A. CUP (Sixth Round Proper)
SATURDAY, 30th MARCH, 1963
Norwich City v. Leicester City
PRICE 6d. EACH

The FA Cup match with Leicester City in 1963 saw the Canaries draw a record crowd of 43,984 to Carrow Road

were the superior side and, try as they might, the Canaries could not break them down. Leicester scored twice and Norwich were looking for a way back with about ten minutes left to play when we were awarded a penalty, right down in front of us. But, to our dismay, Allcock blasted it over the bar and Gordon Banks (England World Cup goalkeeper of three years later) was not required to make a save! It was a disappointing end to a disappointing match, though it had drawn a record crowd of almost 44,000 – most of whom were in our way as we tried to leave after the final whistle.

We eventually arrived back at the college at about six o'clock in the evening, only to find the gates securely locked and Sid's Morris Minor standing forlornly in the middle of the car park! We spent another hour locating the caretaker, who insisted on eating his tea before cycling back to open the gates. As we headed back to Lynn, Sid bemoaned our fate, which he claimed was a judgement on us for missing the afternoon study session. I felt the judgement had been made much earlier, when the Canaries failed, for once, to live up to our expectations of them.

Readers will be pleased to know that despite our inexcusable behaviour, we both passed our examinations – indeed I won a prize for my marks. Our employers were none the wiser about our indiscretion, but we would have exchanged it all to have seen our favourites win their way into the semi-final, whatever the consequences.

16

Nothing to lose

Manchester United 1–2 Norwich City ⚽ FA Cup fourth round ⚽ 18 February 1967

By Dave Stringer

Dave spent a long and illustrious career at Carrow Road, joining the club as a defender in 1965, taking on a variety of coaching roles in the '80s and finally becoming Manager in 1987. Dave retired from the position of Assistant Academy Director in 2001.

There are so many great City matches to recall. However, I would have to select City's giant-killing act at Old Trafford in 1967 as my most memorable moment.

From the moment we were paired with United, who were running away with the First Division at the time, the whole city was caught up in the excitement of the tie. To be honest, we were a mediocre Second Division side with no real form. We were also without the services of our leading goalscorer, Lawrie Sheffield, and very few people gave us any chance at all.

There were some 12,000 City fans among the 63,405 crowd. They were looking for a repeat of the Canaries' 1958/59 FA Cup victory, and also wanted to savour the skills of George Best, Denis Law, John Aston, Bobby Charlton and Nobby Stiles.

It was by far the biggest crowd I had ever played in front of. There was a tremendous atmosphere, but it was also very intimidating. I was marking George Best, but it was really a case of every man for himself. As underdogs we had nothing to lose, but United came at us so strongly we hardly managed to get out of our half. It was real 'backs to the wall' stuff.

After surviving the early onslaught, we stunned the packed crowd by taking a twenty-sixth minute lead. Tommy Bryceland and Gordon Bolland combined to release Don Heath, and as United appealed for offside he calmly slotted the ball past Alex Stepney. That gave us something to cling on to. We had a lead to defend and had ruffled their feathers, but a draw remained our most realistic hope.

Unfortunately Denis Law scored a brilliant equaliser just nine minutes later. It was one of the best goals I had ever seen. After that the game continued in the same vein, with only the outstanding goalkeeping of Kevin Keelan keeping United at bay, until City regained the lead after sixty-five minutes. On one of our rare breaks, the United defence got in a terrible muddle. An intended backpass went beyond Alex Stepney and allowed

Seen here as City boss, Dave recalls the FA Cup win at Old Trafford in 1967 from his playing days

Gordon Bolland to roll the ball into an empty net. The last twenty or so minutes were frantic as we resorted to just hacking the ball away, which in turn only created more pressure, but we managed to hold on to the final whistle.

A disappointing home defeat by Sheffield Wednesday in the next round ended City's cup run, but I have nothing but fond memories of that day at Old Trafford. It was a tremendous occasion. To beat one of Europe's top teams on their ground was a real thrill, and although they were beaten, United arranged for champagne to be sent to the restaurant where we stopped for a meal on the way home, which was a nice gesture.

17

Old Trafford legends humbled

Manchester United 1–2 Norwich City ⚽ FA Cup fourth round ⚽ 18 February 1967

By Russell Parker

While Russell's most treasured memory is of the Canaries' giant-killing exploits at Old Trafford in 1967, his first match was a Division Three home game against Reading on 29 August 1959.

I have supported Norwich since 1959, when my dad had taken me to my first match in the old Division Three (South) against Reading, which we won four-two. My very first football memories, however, are of watching the 1958 FA Cup Final when Aston Villa beat Manchester United with two goals from Peter McParland, and the tragic Munich air disaster.

At the time of this game I was in my last year at CNS. I had already been to a number of away matches, including a trip to The Den to play Millwall. We failed to end their long unbeaten home run, going down two-nil. In fact so far I had never seen Norwich win away!

You can imagine how delighted I was when we drew Manchester United in the Cup, particularly in view of my early footballing memories. I was really just looking forward to the trip to Old Trafford – I didn't anticipate in my wildest dreams what would turn out to be a famous victory.

At that time the Canaries were lingering perilously close to the bottom of the old Second Division, whereas United were about to win the First, and would memorably go on to win the European Cup the next season. Their team boasted football greats such as Bobby Charlton, Denis Law and George Best, and although we had the likes of Terry Allcock, Kevin Keelan, Tommy Bryceland and a young David Stringer, they were hardly household names.

On the day we set out early for the eight-hour coach trip up to Manchester. The talk was that as many as 10,000 fans were making the trip, so it seemed that almost every coach in the county – many of them looking distinctly creaky – was heading for Lancashire that day.

When we parked near Old Trafford there were yellow and green colours everywhere. It seemed that everyone was wearing scarves and rosettes; many were carrying traditional rattles. Indeed I still have the rosette I bought on that day. Clutching my precious ticket, for which I had paid the princely sum of twelve shillings and sixpence, and which I also still have, I passed through the terrace turnstile. In those days it was necessary to get into the ground early to get a place on the terraces, so the time was about 12.30pm. Inside was the incredible sight of a mass of yellow and green filling one whole side of the Old Trafford.

The programme from the Canaries' shock cup win at Old Trafford

The atmosphere was unbelievable. Here I was, in one of the most famous stadiums in Britain, one of a crowd of over 63,000. I took a long look around to convince myself I was there before settling down to read the match programme.

Kick-off came, and rather than being over-awed by the Reds, City actually played rather well. Indeed, the legendary George Best was made to look ordinary, and their defence, marshalled by goalkeeper Alex Stepney, were looking distinctly jittery. So it came as no surprise to the City fans when Don Heath, who was only playing in the absence of Laurie Sheffield, picked up a brilliant Tommy Bryceland through-ball and scored the opening goal. The whole terrace erupted, and for some time 'On the ball, City' drowned out the now-subdued 'Come on you Reds'.

It was time for United to show the Division Two upstarts what football was all about, and they responded with what I still consider the best goal I have ever seen. John Ryan sped down the right wing and put in a cross at about shoulder height to Denis Law, who in a single movement leapt up and scissor-kicked the ball into the roof of the net. Kevin Keelan didn't stand a chance, and now it was the turn of the United hordes to erupt, with a sea of red and white scarves waving at the notorious Stretford End and the famous chants roaring out. Now United would steamroller City into submission, or so they thought. But more drama was to unfold.

A long ball was punted forward for the ever-willing Gordon Bolland to chase. Following a dreadful mix-up between David Sadler and Alex Stepney, the ball squirted clear and Bolland suddenly found himself with the ball in front of a gaping open goal. Afterwards he said that he could not believe his luck as he followed through and simply rolled the ball home to put the Canaries in front at two-one. And that was how the score stayed – Norwich had beaten the team who would later be crowned Division One champions.

What a shock we had when we went back to our coaches. Mine was all right, but many went home that night with smashed windows. The Norwich fans didn't let it stop them celebrating and signing all the way home though.

We eventually arrived home at about 2am. With about a mile to walk home after getting off the coach, I was most worried to hear footsteps behind me in the dark. Concerned that I was being followed, I hurried home and rushed into the house. It was not until the next morning that I was to find out that my pursuer was a friend who had been on the coach behind me, trying to catch me up to discuss the match!

We've got a team in yellow and green

Manchester United 1–2 Norwich City ☾ FA Cup fourth round ☾ 18 February 1967

By Ian Gibson

Despite being born north of the Border, Ian Gibson, MP for Norwich North since 1997, has been a regular at Carrow Road for more than thirty-seven years. His love of football extends to playing in the 'all conquering Parliamentary team'.

Ian Gibson names the Canaries' 2–1 win at Old Trafford as his favourite City game

There is no doubt about my favourite game. The Canaries beat Man United in 1967 and I was there in Manchester. Expecting to be stuffed by Law, Best and Charlton, what a surprise to be returning to Norwich with high hopes of another cup run.

I first heard of Norwich as a young student in Edinburgh, through the 1959 cup run, and ended up here in 1965 at the new University. I attended my first home game at Carrow Road at the invitation of Sir Arthur South on my first weekend.

I confess I came from a strong Scotland football background, but that was a time when Scots players came to England – our annual dreaded enemy. My teams were Queen of the South (from Dumfries) and Celtic, and as well as playing every Saturday I would watch either whenever I could. But after more than thirty years in Norwich I am a Canary through and through.

I work with Bryan and Susan Gunn on their Leukaemia Appeal and visit Carrow Road as a season ticket holder. I also run the Canaries at Westminster group and make sure the great and powerful know where Norwich is and how our team stands poised for the Premiership.

That day in Manchester will always live with me. I remember the train journey up with Michael and John Balls, the vast support for United and running on the pitch to remonstrate with policemen who were apprehending two young Norwich fans for planting balloons on the centre spot. It was a very long day but gosh, how a victory cheers you up. Needless to say, I felt the opposite after Cardiff.

I do think Norwich should aim for the Premiership. We are moving on and we need to be ambitious. There is young footballing talent in the county. We should seek out the stars through our Academy and build a team like the one that played in yellow and green in the San Siro stadium. Big money doesn't always produce the best team!

19

A day to remember

Norwich City 1–3 Sheffield Wednesday 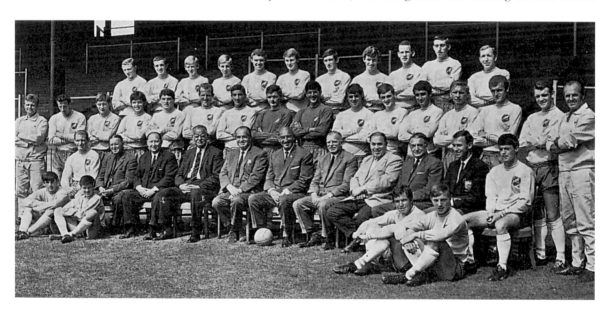 FA Cup fifth round 11 March 1967

By Tony Chapman

More than 30 years of living in Australia have not dimmed Tony's memories of the Canary performances that he enjoyed in the mid '60s.

I remember going to this match with my father as a young lad. The crowd was over 40,000 that day, and we struggled to get a vantage point coming into the ground at the Barclay End. Eventually we climbed up onto a paling fence at the top of the concrete steps that led up to the top of the Barclay.

Sheffield Wednesday were high flyers in the First Division at the time and City were mid-table in the Second. City had beaten Manchester United at Old Trafford in the previous round, and the ground was buzzing for this match.

The squad line up for the camera ahead of the 1966/67 campaign

Unfortunately for City we went down three-one, but it was a day to remember. Players like Kevin Keelan and Tommy Bryceland were outstanding, although Kevin handed Wednesday one of their goals.

Several months after this game our family emigrated to Melbourne, Australia. I still miss Carrow Road after all these years.

20

A great day

Norwich City 3–0 Charlton Athletic ◌ Second Division ◌ 27 December 1971

By Peter Silvester

Thirty-seven goals in 113 senior games is the record of an excellent striker. That was Peter Silvester's record during his four and a half years at Carrow Road. Unfortunately for Peter, just as his goals were propelling the Canaries to Division One for the first time in their history, he suffered a knee injury that kept him out of first-team action for nearly two years.

My most memorable match comes from the 1971/72 campaign. It was against Charlton on Boxing Day. The Canaries had just signed free-scoring Phil Hubbard from Lincoln City on Christmas Eve. There was a crowd of over 30,000 inside Carrow Road and it was really a tremendous occasion. We won quite easily, I scored, and it was just a great day.

I can recall the ball being played up to me. I dummied to go one way, went the other and fired a left-foot shot into the roof of the net. Things were really going well for me that season. The goal was my twelfth in twenty-odd league games and I was enjoying my football.

Three games later, my luck changed. I was jumping for a high ball when I felt my knee go in mid-air. I didn't land awkwardly or anything, it just went. Unfortunately the knee did not swell up and was not diagnosed as having cartilage damage immediately. I trained on it a few times but then it gave up completely. It was very disappointing to miss out on the rest of that season.

My favourite ever goal was also against Charlton – my lucky team. It was a low volley from about thirty yards. Graham Paddon sent in a cross and I just went for it – the ball never went more than two feet off the ground as it flew in. Then there was a header at Hull that featured in Match of the Day's Goal of the Month competition in 1971/72. It was a straightforward near-post header, but it came at the end of an excellent build-up.

Peter is welcomed to City Hall during the 1971/72 reunion weekend

An electric atmosphere

Birmingham City 4–0 Norwich City 🌍 Second Division 🌍 4 March 1972

By Tony Harper

While Tony here recalls a memorable defeat of 1972, his first Canary experience was in 1962 when Norwich City drew 1–1 with Bury at Carrow Road.

On a bright Saturday morning in late winter, our motley crew congregated at Thorpe Station, names that spring to mind from the group include Mike, Richard, Bill, Ollie, Julian, Ivan, Derek and my brother David. I wonder how many of those characters are still Canary fans after all these years.

Most of us were part of the lively and noisy South Stand of that period, although we were happy to be accompanied by one or two River End moaners. It was hardly surprising that our fervour was building: City were top of the old Second Division, with every prospect of reaching the dreamland of the First Division for the first time in their history. Carrow Road crowds had risen to well over 20,000, and the Canary Special was riding on a wave of enthusiasm as it pulled away from Thorpe that morning. Our destination was St Andrews and a meeting with Birmingham, who were beginning to build a run of decent results themselves and had moved up to fourth in the table – six points behind the Canaries.

Such was the feeling of invincibility instilled by manager Ron Saunders at that time that the talk on the train was not so much of whether City would be promoted, but who would accompany us in second place. Opinion was divided between Birmingham and Millwall, who had been breathing down our necks all season. Most of us hoped it would be Birmingham, as none of us liked Millwall, although I recall Bill saying he would prefer it the other way round as it would make things easier in our struggle for First Division survival next season. What an optimist!

We arrived at New Street Station and walked the mile or so to St Andrews. It was only my third or fourth away game, so I was happy to follow those who had made the trip before. Unlike my previous away trips, there seemed to be a real buzz in the air, heightened by a verbal exchange with a passing busload of home supporters.

As we approached the ground, the anticipation grew. We made our way across open wasteland to the Railway End. Here, at the turnstiles, we were greeted by a queue of City fans snaking back for several hundred yards, while from inside the ground a loud chorus of 'On the ball, City' sent shivers down our spines. It seemed like the whole of Norwich had turned out. Once inside, we shuffled along an already-packed terrace towards the goal and finally settled in a spot just

The programme from the Canaries' 4–0 thrashing at St Andrews in March 1972

inside the penalty area. My first impression was that St Andrews seemed rather run-down, but what it lacked in grandeur it made up for in sheer size. Behind our terrace, packed with City fans, was a seated stand. To the left was a simple grandstand with a seated paddock in front, while the opposite end was a covered terrace. However, our attention was drawn to the vast covered terrace to the right, Birmingham's Kop, rapidly filling up with home supporters.

The atmosphere was electric. The players emerged, greeted by a crescendo of sound: 'On the ball City' ringing out from our terrace and 'Keep right on till the end of the road' from the rest of the ground. City fans were surprised to see a new striker in the number eight shirt: Jim Bone, making his debut following his signing from Partick Thistle for the now-paltry sum of £30,000.

The pitch was already wet and heavy as the match kicked off, and it rapidly deteriorated further and became waterlogged as rain gave way to a heavy snowstorm. City started brightly though, and fans hoped that Saunders' side, renowned for their fitness and stamina, would have little trouble adapting to the conditions. Unfortunately City got completely bogged down in the mud, and Birmingham, who had their own powerful forwards in Bob Latchford and Bob Hatton, combined with the emerging silky skills of Trevor Francis, took complete control. Meanwhile, at the other end, the City forwards had little success against the physical Birmingham defence. The back line was typified by the Birmingham centre half, Roger Hynd, who had the presence of an oak tree. The City fans continued their excellent support throughout the match, but it was never going to be our day, and it was left to the Birmingham supporters in the bumper crowd of nearly 41,000 to raise the roof.

The walk back to the station was a bit of a drudge, feeling cold and wet with the rain still falling and the thoughts of a four-nil defeat hanging heavy. Back at the relative warmth and comfort of New Street, we boarded the Canary Special and were in sombre mood, as in the distance, St Andrews could be seen gradually diminishing in the murky gloom as we sat quietly reflecting on what might have been. But by the time we arrived back at Thorpe station, our mood had lightened, and our group even managed a chorus of 'and now you're going to believe us, we only lost four-nil...'

The result that day turned out to be only a minor setback, as the Canaries did eventually win the championship and hence promotion to the top flight for the first time ever. Birmingham joined us in second place. To me, the result of the match was a disaster, but the occasion was unforgettable, with a volume of noise and overall atmosphere that I have never since experienced at an away match.

22

Worship for Graham

Norwich City 5–1 Blackpool ☾ Second Division ☾ 25 March 1972

By John McNamara

There may have been no goals on John's first visit to Carrow Road (QPR, 2 October 1971), but here he recalls what was for him a magical first season as a Canaries fan.

I'm sure my sister fancied him. She seemed delighted by my sudden nagging attention. She came over all giggly, animated, kind of nice, really. Not like my sister at all. 'Yes, that's right. Graham Paddon drinks in the Mustard Pot after a game. I can get you his autograph. But what's it worth?' she said.

I'm not sure what I promised – probably the earth – but she duly obliged as Dad parked carefully outside the small pub, a familiar landmark on the way back to Great Yarmouth. 'Are you sure about this?' he asked impatiently, eyeing up the long line of eastbound traffic in his rear view mirror.

'I'm sure.' Gloria said. 'All the players go there after the game. Everyone knows.' She scampered across Thorpe Road and disappeared inside the pub. How I wished I could too, but at eleven years of age, some things were beyond even my powers of persuasion. Dad sat tapping his fingers on the steering wheel, no doubt pondering the wisdom of encouraging his daughter to rush into pubs on the lookout for men she had never met. After a few minutes, Gloria reappeared and skipped joyfully (it seemed to me) back to the car.

As Dad drove off I waited. She said nothing. 'Well, did you get it?' I almost howled in despair.

'No.' I felt the sting of tears welling up behind my eyes, the pain of disappointment deep inside. As we drove away, slowly now in the post-match traffic, I felt a kind of lonesome anguish.

'I got Kenny Foggo, Peter Sylvester and Maxie Briggs though!' I looked up in disbelief. 'And David Cross!' I can't remember my exact words, but actions speak louder anyway. I think I kissed her. She giggled some more before handing back my newly signed programme.

This was just one of many highlights in a year filled with wonder. My first game of football – QPR – replete with a genuine superstar, Rodney Marsh, but sadly no goals. The priceless memories of Dad and me occasionally catching the Seagull coach at Yarmouth seafront on match days, and talking with other dads and sons who we didn't know but who soon became friendly faces on the short, thrilling journey to Carrow Road. My dad holding my hand, the only time I can remember him doing this, as we walked across the railway bridge before the game, with excitement growing and the sun shining in our eyes, stopping briefly to get a programme outside the Clarence Harbour. Or weaving our way among the crowds to the hopelessly busy chip shop after the game. Memories of a new-found identity. Memories of being top of the table – and staying there, through thick and thin. And memories of Graham Paddon – the greatest.

My mother would smile. She loved the fact my dad and me had a new bond, and she took genuine, unselfish delight in our tales of heroism, and very occasional disappointment, when we got home during that beautiful, shimmering season. Looking back now, I reflect on the millions of men like dad

Jimmy Bone celebrates his goal against Blackpool in March 1972

and me, and I understand this crazy, immoral, passionate game, and its illogical hold on the male psyche. A special bond indeed.

Preston North End, Luton, the big one against Millwall (they had had the audacity to beat us at the Den), Birmingham and Hull, it just kept getting better and better. And then, to me, the greatest game: Norwich–Blackpool. It had never occurred to me that teams could take beatings like this. That one set of eleven individuals had the desire, heart and unity to inflict such suffering. I knew then that I would always be a fan.

Graham Paddon was crowned king that day, his late, trademark left-footer from twenty-five yards after Kenny Foggo squared the ball from the right wing screamed into the net at the River End, and the place went mad. A perfect game. Bone, Foggo and Cross scored – but Paddon got two. To me, he was Bobby Charlton, Johnny Giles and Rodney Marsh all rolled into one. When Paddon scored a hat-trick against Arsenal, at Highbury, in the League Cup quarter-final later that year, I knew he was a god. Away team players just didn't score three goals there. All these years later I have yet to see a player who could better Paddon on form. I might be biased, but I've seen Cruyff, Hoddle, Souness, Brady and Beckham play live, and it's true, they're all legends. But I never had an emotional link to any of them. When I saw Graham Paddon dominate a game, it was special. It was personal.

Those early years, as champions, and then playing for the first time in the top flight, left Dad and me with some golden memories. I still remember the excitement of Martin Peters' arrival. I remember too staring in disbelief as Justin Fashanu teed up and then unleashed the finest volley Carrow Road had ever seen, in an eight-goal thriller with Liverpool that Phil Neal later described as the best game of football he ever played in. I was there for that Milk Cup semi-final win over Ipswich too. The picture of Steve Bruce wheeling away after scoring, with Donowa, Channon and Deehan in hot pursuit, is probably the greatest sports photo ever taken. Memories so good, you don't ever have to think about the bad times.

Dave Stringer's stylish team, and the Mike Walker years, when – let's face it – we, and the rest of Britain, just couldn't believe how good we really were. The memory of Bayern Munich at home will live with me forever, as will the disappointment of not being able to get a ticket for Inter Milan.

I spoke last year to a friend of mine, who had met Graham Paddon several times at one of Caister-On-Sea's finer hostelries. He told me how Graham had naturally been inconsolable when his mother had died, and how moving and poignant it was for him to discover his mum had for years kept press cuttings of all his matches in scrapbooks, unbeknown to the great man himself. 'He realised then what his achievements had meant to other people, and he was genuinely shocked,' said my friend. I apologise for intruding on another man's private feelings. But I do it safe in the knowledge that he intruded on mine. Yes, Graham, you were worshipped.

23

Vital victory

Norwich City 1–0 Swindon Town ⚽ Second Division ⚽ 22 April 1972

By Duncan Forbes

Duncan Forbes has a special place in the hearts of all Norwich City supporters. After joining the Canaries in October 1968 as a utility player, he quickly impressed the fans with his enthusiasm and commitment to the game. Ron Saunders made him captain and his leadership qualities helped guide the club through an historic era as First Division football was brought to Carrow Road for the first time, and Wembley was reached on two occasions. After hanging up his boots, he joined the Commercial Department as Shop Manager and Sales Manager before his old defensive partner, Dave Stringer, appointed him as Chief Scout in 1987, a role he held until his retirement in 2001.

Duncan heads home the only goal of the game against Swindon Town

The last home match of the 1971/72 Second Division championship-winning season against Swindon was the most memorable match of my long career. We had lost at Middlesborough the previous week and there was plenty of anxiety in the camp. I had scored the only goal in our previous home match, against Sheffield Wednesday, and was able to repeat that feat in this match. It was a pretty uninspiring match until my 'classic' header just before half-time.

We had won a corner that was only partially cleared out to our left flank. I stayed up in attack, Graham Paddon delivered a perfect cross, and my header rocketed into the top left-hand corner. No goalkeeper in the world would have saved that!

The victory was vital, setting up the thrilling finale to the season with two games at Orient and Watford. With these three games, promotion and then the Championship were won in a period of just eight days.

Very few players within our squad had any First Division experience and we all desperately wanted to play in it. When I arrived at Norwich there was no telling how my career would take off. I was lucky to be in the right place at the right time as Norwich made great steps forward as a club.

A piece of history

Leyton Orient 1–2 Norwich City ☾ Second Division ☾ 24 April 1972

By Kathy Blake

As Norwich City's FA Cup run came to an end with their fifth-round defeat by Sheffield Wednesday on 11 March 1967, Kathy was on the Carrow Road stands experiencing her first taste of Canary fever. Despite the result their performance inspired Kathy to become a committed and die-hard fan.

The programme from the promotion-winning night at Brisbane Road

There have been many memorable, more outstanding achievements since this match, but I have chosen it because it was the very first time we achieved what I had always thought of as the unattainable promised land of the First Division.

After a shaky patch towards the end of the season, we had defeated Swindon Town one-nil the previous Saturday. This left us needing just two points from our remaining two games away at Orient and Watford.

At the time there was no Club Canary, and away travel was a hit-and-miss affair run by Mascot Coaches. The buses left from Bell Avenue, which is now underneath Castle Mall. We had to leave at noon for a 7.30pm kick-off. The A11 in those days was a long single carriageway that snaked its way through every minor concentration of population between Norwich and the outskirts of north London, and the journey was long and tedious.

This was one of several occasions when I bunked off school to watch Norwich City play. Nowadays, I have trouble looking my teenage son in the eye and telling him with any conviction that he cannot skip school to watch midweek away matches.

The match itself was a very tense affair. Goals from Ken Foggo and a penalty from Graham Paddon clinched the victory, but I spent the last ten minutes watching through my fingers, something I still do today

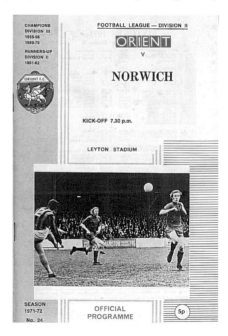

when things get tight. At the end we all invaded the pitch. This was customary in those days and carried no threat of being banned. I will admit now to pulling up the penalty spot from which Paddon had scored. I still have it in my possession today, although thirty years on it looks more like an ounce of Golden Virginia than anything associated with a football stadium. But I know what it is.

25

Winning the league

Watford 1–1 Norwich City ☾ Second Division ☾ 29 April 1972

By Geoffrey Belson

Geoffrey's first match at Carrow Road coincided with their 1968 fourth-round FA Cup defeat by Southampton, when Ron Davies, who had left the Canaries for Saints two seasons earlier, scored one of the goals that sealed their fate.

I have many happy memories of supporting Norwich, and one I shall never forget is the last match of our title-winning season, against Watford at Vicarage Road.

Watford themselves were bottom of the league, while we had already secured promotion by beating Leyton Orient in a midweek game that I had to miss because of work commitments.

There was a huge contingent of Norwich fans at Watford and only a very small group of Watford supporters. The atmosphere was electric – it was almost like being at Carrow Road. We were put in the uncovered end of the ground by the local police, and the heavens opened and it poured. Soaking wet, we glanced towards the other end of the ground to see it was only quarter-full – the few Watford supporters in attendance taunting us for getting wet.

Suddenly, about ten Norwich supporters leaped over the fence and ran towards the other end of the ground. 'Excellent idea,' we thought, and before you knew what had happened the whole contingent of Norwich supporters was running across the pitch, completely outnumbering the police, who gave in and just watched. The Watford supporters ran for their lives and disappeared out of the end of the stand to be put into another stand.

I got right at the front of the stand and my photo was taken and ended up on the front of the Eastern Daily Press special supplement.

The match was not a great one, but that didn't matter – we had won the league for the first time ever, and I was lucky enough to be there to witness this great era. Dave Stringer's goal at Watford had made history, and we celebrated all the way back to Norwich. The city was buzzing for days after.

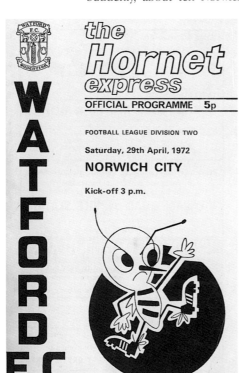

The programme from the Canaries' championship-winning trip to Vicarage Road

26

Come on you reds!

Watford 1–1 Norwich City ◐ Second Division ◐ 29 April 1972

By Glen Sandell

Like so many City fans, Glen Sandell recalls the climate of the 71/72 season as his favourite period of following the Canaries fortunes.

Saturday 29 April 1972 is a date forever ingrained in my memory. I was only ten at the time, and this was to be my first ever away match. My best friend's dad had got us all tickets. The excitement of the day began with the journey down to London, the road awash with yellow and green banners and scarves being flown with pride from coaches and cars alike. The weather, though, was fairly bad, with heavy rain on and off all the way down.

During the season the home vocal support had been good, but what a sound greeted our ears as we queued outside with hordes of the yellow and green army – I'd never heard 'On the ball, City' sung so loudly. Goose-bumps ran down my spine and the hairs on the back of neck stood up – as they do to this day when I hear that song at away grounds.

Once inside the ground we were greeted by an open-ended stand at our end, and behind the other goal a stand that looked very similar to our beloved Barclay. The two side stands were old and a bit higgledy-piggledy. The pitch was looking very sorry for itself, with not much grass to be seen – just mud, glorious mud everywhere.

This was Watford's best home gate of the season by quite some way: 22,410, with the Norwich support making up at least two-thirds of the total. The poor Watford fans, who had been relegated to the Third Division several weeks earlier, had very little to sing about. They did, however, make a big mistake when, after a bit of backward and forward banter, the skies opened and the rain teemed down once again. They could be heard to sing 'If you want us come and get us,' and this was just the cue the Norwich fans needed to climb over the fence and run across the pitch towards the other end. As a few hundred turned into a few thousand, the Watford end emptied and was proudly taken over by Ron Saunders' green and yellow army.

The poor overworked Tannoy announcer kept appealing for spectators to stay off the already-bad pitch before it became unplayable. My friend's dad, being a respectable man, did not think it right to mount the fence, so we stayed where we were in the uncovered end. At least we were able to get to the front and take up many a child's favourite spot – sitting with legs through the barrier fence.

As it was my first away game I had a slight shock when the teams took to the

Thirty years on and the 1971/72 squad are reunited as part of the Canaries' Centenary celebrations

1972

pitch – why I can't see a team in yellow and green? I was soon put right and joined in the unusual chant of 'Come on you reds'.

By now the despondent home supporters, who had lost their place in Division Two and now their nice dry stand as well, had moved into the open terrace behind us and kept us amused with chants of 'going down'. Our end now contained a mixture of home and away supporters, and one or two minor scuffles broke out, but nothing serious.

The game itself flew by, with our footballing skills rather hampered by the mud. We were one-nil up at half time, but David Stringer's goal was cancelled out in the second half by a Watford equaliser. Nevertheless, I had witnessed a bit of Norwich City history, as we were crowned Champions of Division Two and proudly awaited our place in Division One for the first time ever.

Forever on the ball City.

1972

27

We took the Rookery

Watford 1–1 Norwich City ⚽ Second Division ⚽ 29 April 1972

By Martin Thirkettle

While Martin describes the exodus of some 17,000 City fans to sunny Hertfordshire to witness the Club become the champions of Division Two, his first match, a 0–0 draw with Leyton Orient in September 1964, also drew a respectable attendance of over 20,000. However, that season's final result was certainly less satisfying, with the Canaries finishing sixth in Division Two.

How do you begin the story of probably the largest exodus of Norwich fans ever to travel to an away league fixture, one that is still remembered by both Norwich and Watford fans to this day? On a cloudy, wet April morning, an estimated 17,000 City fans (out of a total crowd of just over 22,000) made the relatively short trip to Vicarage Road to see the lads grab the point that confirmed them as Second Division champions and took them into the top flight for the first time in the club's history.

At the beginning of the season we were totally unfancied to get anywhere near the promotion placings, having ended up in only the tenth spot the previous season. However, by the time the middle of October came round, and we hadn't lost one of our opening thirteen games, things were beginning to look decidedly tasty. David Cross, Peter Silvester and Kenny Foggo were regularly putting the goals away, and crowds were consistently pushing above 20,000. There were some dodgy moments, like losing four-nil at Birmingham and one-nil at Middlesbrough. But by the time we were heading for Watford, we had played (and won) our last home game of the season in front of over 31,000 fans against Swindon, and followed that by sealing promotion against Orient on an emotional Monday night before the trip to Vicarage Road. All we needed now was a point at Watford to secure the title.

The exodus to Watford for the expected celebrations was comprehensive. Every single coach in Norfolk appeared to be heading south along the A11, including some that looked like their previous excursion had been carrying the members of the St Trinian's cast on location. Fully laden 'Black Cat', 'Cullings' and 'Mascot' coaches were hitting the tarmac, on the road to promotion. Two friends, Chris Conroy and Paul Ballard, and myself had joined schoolmates on a coach that had begun its trip in Aylsham and its life in the Jurassic period.

Especially for the occasion, I had commandeered a bedsheet from Mum, which we had dyed yellow and emblazoned with the immortal legend 'NORWICH CITY – CHAMPIONS DIV. 2' in sprayed-on Austin 1100 green. With weather conditions likely to test our dye to the limit, we boarded the coach at The Boundary pub and sang our way into the depths of Hertfordshire.

On arrival in Watford, a police escort met us, which was beginning to become an all-too-common feature of away travel at that time. On this occasion, however, the police were not the unsmiling, uncommunicative bunch of miseries that kept travelling fans company during the 70s and 80s. No, this lot were worse – a bunch of sad, totally humourless automatons who could have competed with the Terminator in their emotionless, mindless devotion to duty. We had hardly set foot off the coach before we were brusquely informed that we were likely to get nicked for even thinking about singing on the way to the ground. This attitude may have had something to do with the fact that Watford were on their way back to Division Three, whence they had come in 1969, while we were heading for greater things in the opposite direction. Whatever the reason, they were unable to spoil our buoyant mood.

Once in the ground, we took up a spot about three-quarters of the way up the open terrace, right behind the goal, facing the empty Rookery End. It was about an hour before the game, but the end that held Norwich fans was already getting to the heaving, swaying stage – the incessant rain becoming more of a blessing than a curse. The pitch itself looked as though it should have been hosting the World Mud Wrestling Championship rather than a football match, as the rain, which by now was continuous and heavy, was turning the playing surface into a quagmire. This, however, did not affect the party atmosphere of the travelling support as more and more banners, scarves and balloons were appearing at our end of the ground. Through the veil of precipitation it was still difficult to see more than a handful of Watford supporters cosily enjoying the moisture-free environment of their covered end.

The City squad that brought First Division football to Norwich for the first time in the Club's history

It was about this time that the rain decided to turn monsoon and a small group of Norwich fans decided to run on to the middle of the pitch and place a couple of yellow and green balloons close to the centre spot, roared on by the packed away end. Unsurprisingly, the humourless local Plod took great delight in escorting the perpetrators from the ground, while totally ignoring a band of Watford fans that had emerged from the gloom to stamp on the balloons and leg it unhindered back to their end. The endless need for justice being what it is, more Norwich fans ran onto the pitch bearing balloons while others ran about acting as decoys to the police. Suddenly, the idea of running onto the pitch, or more precisely, the idea of heading across it towards the comfort of the Rookery End, caught hold like some great Biblical epidemic. Not only was the pitch alive with Doc Marten-wearing skinheads, but also Norwich fans of every age, gender and disposition were heading for the Rookery.

The sight of thousands of Norwich fans, some of pensionable age and some carrying kids, heading towards Watford fans temporarily frozen in terror before leaping out over the turnstiles, is as vivid to me today as it was then. The scale of this exodus meant the police could do little about it and, despite the intimidating nature of the situation, it was accompanied by very little violence.

So within minutes the Rookery End was echoing to the chant of 'We took the Rookery (Easy! easy!)' and thousands of Norwich fans (including myself, Chris and Paul) were getting nicely dry. The open end continued, meanwhile, to fill up with more of our compatriots, still trying to get onto the terrace for a good view of what we all hoped would be a historic occasion for the club.

When the teams took the field to a deafening roar (from the Norwich fans at least), the first thing that confronted us was the spectacle of Norwich wearing an all-red kit – something that had never happened before, and has only happened again recently as an experiment. Frankly, we didn't care what the team were wearing – they could have turned out and played naked for all we cared – all we were worried about was the one point needed to secure the Championship. In this respect, we were not to be denied. Watford's equaliser to Dave Stringer's first half goal made the last few minutes incredibly nerve-wracking, but the party erupted at the final whistle. The players were swamped in a mass of fans that had spent the last ten minutes of the game hugging the touchline, much as you'd see at Sloughbottom Park on a Sunday morning.

The post-match celebrations passed in a blur of joy. In response to the fans' vociferous requests, the team mounted what passed for Watford's equivalent of a Directors' Box and proceeded to throw their shirts out to the adoring hordes. The lad standing next to me caught Duncan Forbes' number five shirt and proudly put it on, despite the fact that it was covered in mud and sweat. Wherever he is today, I hope that he still has that shirt and has the chance to dig it out occasionally to revere it, and the memory of that historic day.

28

A convert to the cause

Arsenal 0–3 Norwich City ☘ League Cup fifth round ☘ 21 November 1972

By Susan Gorman

Perhaps uniquely amongst the contributors of these 100 great moments, Susan is a Canaries convert – here describing the 90 minutes that transformed her from a Gunners fan. Her allegiance to the Club has not waned in thirty years; despite living in Essex and leading a very busy life she is still a regular in the Lower Barclay stand.

On a cold November night in north London I stood on the terraces of North Bank, Highbury, home of Arsenal FC, with my husband-to-be Brian (to whom I am still married) and my mum. The anticipation was mounting – what would we see from Norwich City FC, newly promoted Second Division champions? As we had not travelled to the away game at Carrow Road in September, we did not know what to expect.

The teams entered the arena and the game commenced. I had been an Arsenal supporter for many years, watching them through the European Fairs Cup and the double year of 1970–71, but after ninety minutes I was a Norwich City supporter. Norwich, in their distinctive yellow and green, played their socks off – with enthusiasm, guts and a never-say-die attitude.

Brian and Mum could not shut me up all the way home. I was converted.

Graham Paddon's hat-trick at Highbury saw City through to the League Cup semi-final

We eventually moved to Essex and could easily travel to London to watch Arsenal, but my heart is with Norwich and we are proud to be season ticket holders in the Lower Barclay Stand. My mum even looks out for the Norwich results now, which isn't bad for an Arsenal fanatic.

Oh by the way, the score on that cold November night was Arsenal nil, Norwich City three, but whatever the score was, Norwich City FC had another supporter. 'I'm City 'til I die…'

Justice

Norwich City 3–2 Chelsea ☉ League Cup semi-final, second leg ☉ 20 December 1972 (abandoned due to fog)

By Roy Waller

For many Norwich City supporters who cannot get to matches, radio commentaries are the best way to follow their team's best fortunes and Radio Norfolk's Roy Waller is a familiar voice behind the microphone, reporting to listeners on most of the Canaries' home and away matches.

On 20 December 1972 Chelsea visited Carrow Road for the second leg of the League Cup semi-final. This I recall as my most memorable match.

We had won the first leg at Stamford Bridge two-nil with goals from David Cross and Jimmy Bone. The whole city was excited about the prospect of the Canaries playing at Wembley for the first time. As I stood in the packed South Stand, we looked certain to reach the final, leading three-two on the night and five-two on aggregate with just a few minutes to go.

What happened next has become part of Canary folklore. Suddenly the fog descended, making watching and playing the game impossible. Referee Gordon Hill faced an impossible situation, eventually abandoning the match with just six minutes left. As we poured away from the ground, everyone was stunned at the way the prospect of a Wembley appearance had been snatched away.

I have my own pet theory as to why the fog descended so quickly. Russell

Allison always used to unlock the gates about ten minutes from time. I believe that when he did this he allowed the clear air to escape from the stadium which in turn allowed the fog to drop. I spoke to Michael Hunt, the Anglia TV weatherman at the time, and he confirmed that this was possible.

Luckily, justice was seen to be done when a Steve Govier header gave the Canaries a one-nil replay victory to take the club to Wembley.

Roy Waller – the voice of Carrow Road

30

Beaten by the fog

Norwich City 3–2 Chelsea ⚽ League Cup semi-final, second leg ⚽ 20 December 1972 (abandoned due to fog)

By Geoffrey Belson

Chelsea 'take two' – no fog to halt the Canaries' charge this time: the programme for the re-arranged semi-final, second leg

I can remember, as a fourteen-year-old, the joy of watching the Canaries reaching the final of the 1972/73 League Cup final.

In the fifth round, having beaten Leicester at home, Hull City away, and Stockport away, we were drawn against mighty Arsenal away from home. This, I thought, would be our last game in the competition, but instead it became a night to remember. Graham Paddon, with his long, flowing golden locks, became our hero with a fantastic hat-trick. This was fantasy football – we romped home three-nil and Graham made the headlines.

The semi-final was played over two legs, with the first leg away at Stamford Bridge. After Arsenal, sprits were high, and we made the headlines again, winning two-nil with goals from Jimmy Bone and Dave Cross. Tickets for the second leg went on sale during the week, and my friend and I skived off school for the day to queue up. We waited for over two hours in a line that stretched from the ground over the river bridge and beyond. The next day at school we were summoned to the head teacher. Fearing the worst, we approached his office, but of course we'd forgotten that he was a City fan. As we sat before him he just smiled and asked us if we'd managed to get tickets.

The day of the semi-final came and the ground was packed. The atmosphere was electric, with choruses of 'On the ball, City' coming from all stands – even the main stand!

Unbelievably, we played a blinder. We were leading three-two, with goals from Terry Anderson, Dave Cross and Paul Cheesley, when a thick fog came swirling in from the River End. Within minutes we couldn't see the players on the pitch – all that reached us was the sound of the ball being kicked. The whistle blew, and an announcement came over the loudspeakers: the game was to be cancelled and would be replayed.

Our hearts sank. We couldn't believe what was happening– one moment we were so happy, looking forward to Wembley,

NORWICH CITY FOOTBALL CLUB

CANARIES v CHELSEA

Carrow Road, Wednesday, 3rd January, 1973
Kick-off 7.30 pm   League Cup Semi-final (2nd leg)

7p

Official Match-day Programme   Volume 1 Number 18

and the next so sad and confused. Chelsea must have thought this was their lucky day. We went home in a sombre mood, fearing the chance to go to Wembley was gone forever.

We queued for tickets again for the replay, along with half our school – and the teachers too! The second meeting with Chelsea was another great game, and Steve Govier scored the most important goal of his career to take us into the final. It was a dream come true for the people of Norwich. The whole city was buzzing with excitement.

The final against Spurs was a disappointment. We lost one-nil to a Ralph Coates goal, but just being there, seeing Kevin Keelan in goal at Wembley and Duncan Forbes and Dave Stringer gracing the turf, is an experience that I shall never forget.

31

Wembley

Norwich City 0–1 Tottenham Hotspur ⚽ League Cup Final ⚽ 3 March 1973

By Geoff Butler

Geoff Butler played 196 First Team games for the Canaries between 1968 and 1975, an era that included some of Norwich City's most historic moments. During this period the club progressed from being a run-of-the-mill Second Division outfit to win the Second Division Championship, be relegated, and promoted again the following season, as well as reaching Wembley twice in League Cup finals.

My most memorable match was Norwich City's first ever visit to Wembley, when they faced Tottenham in the League Cup Final.

The whole day passed us by very quickly, and despite the fact that we lost one-nil I have some very vivid memories of the occasion. When I think now of the noise that greeted the two teams as they emerged from the tunnel, seeing the thousands of supporters decked out in yellow and green, it still brings out the goose-pimples.

The game itself was not too good; we didn't do ourselves justice at all. Tottenham scored and hit a post, but we had our chances too. I remember hitting a long pass to Graham Paddon who ran on and was bundled over inside the penalty area, but we didn't get a penalty. Duncan Forbes headed over the bar and David Cross went close with an overhead kick.

Looking back at the whole build-up to the final, I believe we didn't concentrate enough on the match. We were so wrapped up in the razzamatazz – being measured for suits, sorting out tickets, conducting countless interviews. We were not used to it, and it sidetracked us from the main event – winning the game. The occasion was so great that it was not until we returned to our hotel

The programme from the Canaries'
first trip to the twin towers

rooms after the game that the realisation that we had lost sunk in.

One amusing moment came as we were on the coach going down Wembley Way before the game. The tension was unbearable, and there was hardly a word being spoken when suddenly Dave Stringer let out a scream. 'I needed that,' he said, and it released some of the tension from all of us.

Another memorable game is the second leg of the 1973 League Cup semi-final, against Chelsea. Anyone who was present when the fog descended at Carrow Road will never forget it. I haven't!

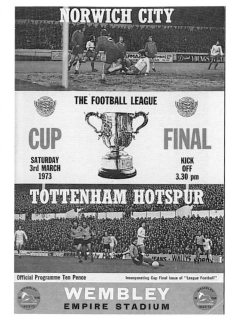

We were about ten minutes from booking a trip to Wembley, leading Chelsea five-two on aggregate. I can remember Gordon Hill, the referee, saying 'there is no way this game won't finish'. He waited for half an hour for the fog to clear, but it wouldn't and he was left with no choice but to abandon the match. Thankfully we won the re-match one-nil.

32

Relegation cliffhanger

Norwich City 2–1 Crystal Palace ● First Division ● 24 April 1973

By Judy Trivett

I have seen at least 1400 competitive matches involving City, and since 1981 I have been a steward on the Club Canary coaches that go to every away match. Following the Canaries also led me to meeting my husband, Mike, in 1973 whilst on a trip to Manchester City. We were married in 1977, and our son Stevie was born in 1981. Stevie is already a well travelled fan, having watched the Canaries play at about forty-five league grounds.

The match that sticks most in my memory has to be the relegation cliffhanger against Crystal Palace at Carrow Road on 24 April 1973. Most of us felt that we

Judy Trivett's family affinity for Norwich City began back in March 1960 when she attended her first ever match, a 0–0 home draw against Bradford City in Division Three. In the 1962/63 season she started going to every home game and by 1966/67, travelling to virtually every Canary away game became part of her weekly routine.

The programme from the crucial 2–1 winner over the Eagles in 1973

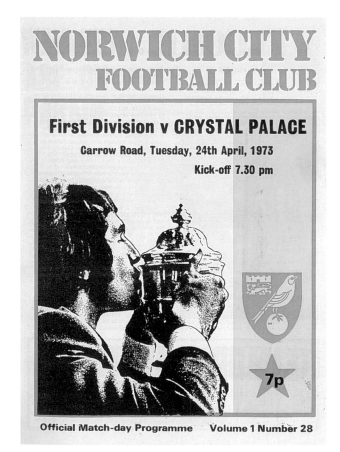

were already doomed going into the busy Easter programme, but our one-nil away win at West Brom on Easter Saturday kicked the door slightly open for us. We lost three-nil at Wolves on Easter Monday, making the Tuesday night game against Palace virtually a 'them or us' decider.

The pressure mounted on City when Don Rogers gave Palace the lead from the penalty spot after Duncan Forbes' foul on Derek Possee. Colin Suggett scored an equaliser fairly soon after as the drama unfolded.

The second half was one-way traffic as we threw everything at them, including Alan Black, who unbelievably found himself clean through on goal at one point. He missed of course!

David Cross then had a goal disallowed as the time raced by. Then, in the last minute, with everyone resigned to a draw, Dave Stringer headed home a free-kick at the River End to send everyone wild.

Reaching the First Division was tremendous and it would have been tragic to have given up our hard-earned status so quickly. The emotion of that night was unforgettable, and the last-minute goal just summoned up the drama of that whole season.

I have plenty of other great memories from my thirty-three years of watching City. Our recent win in Munich has to be one of the greatest nights for any City fan. After waiting so long to compete in Europe, the quality of our performance at such a stadium, against such a team with the whole nation watching us, was a truly proud moment.

The Milk Cup semi-final victory against Ipswich at Carrow Road in 1985 was another great match. The joy of getting to Wembley and preventing Ipswich from doing so at the same time was almost unconfined.

Another match, at Bolton in September 1974, stands out. It was a League Cup tie and one of the first times I can remember a Norwich side completely outplaying the opposition, in terms of style and quality football. It's a stupid game to remember as it ended nil-nil, but it was really the start of an era as far as City were concerned.

33

An emotional rollercoaster

Norwich City 2–1 Crystal Palace ❍ First Division ❍ 24 April 1973

By Nicholas Mead

Nicholas was eight years old when he attended his first Norwich City match and became hooked on the Club. Thirty-three years later his enthusiasm for the team is as strong as ever, although, as he lives in Cornwall, getting to Carrow Road fixtures is a little more difficult than it used to be.

Colin Suggett was on target as the Canaries overcame the Eagles

I became a Norwich City fan on 20 December 1969. To an objective observer it wouldn't seem like a very auspicious occasion – a one-all draw with Sheffield United (Ken Foggo scored, Graham Paddon had one disallowed) fought out in front of just over 7400 fans. I loved it though, and thirty-two years on Carrow Road still feels like home.

In the beginning Norwich City was just my hobby, but the match that turned me from a supporter into a fanatic was a truly titanic struggle that took place a few years later, a week before my twelfth birthday. Everything about the match means that we are unlikely ever to see its like again: the build-up over the preceding seasons, the league situation at the time, the characters involved, and, finally, the way events unfolded on the night itself.

In the early seventies, supporting City was a carefree occupation. It was three years before I saw us lose a home league game – not because I was missing a lot of matches, but because City were virtually unbeatable at Carrow Road. There were only two home defeats in the 1970/71 season and none at all in the famous promotion season. So when the tide turned I really wasn't prepared for it. And in December 1972 it turned with a vengeance: suddenly, the team that couldn't lose became the team that couldn't win.

Why this happened I don't know, but suddenly the team that had beaten Arsenal and Derby County – the reigning champions – couldn't do anything right. Nineteen matches went by without a league win, and we were transformed from European possibilities into relegation certainties. To add to the misery, in the middle of that run we went to Wembley and lost. It seemed as though all the hard work of the previous season, all the glory of that marvellous championship, would come to nothing. It was unbearably sad.

The only bright spots in all of this had been our League Cup semi-finals with Chelsea. Three times we played them, and three times we beat them. So despite our terrible run, when they came to Carrow Road in the penultimate home game of the season we had a realistic chance of beating them again, and we did – one-nil. We were still in desperate trouble though – West Brom, Palace and City were competing to avoid the two relegation spots, so our matches at the Hawthorns and against Palace were going to be crucial. A week after the Chelsea win, City beat West Brom – that just about finished them off, and City and Palace went head-to-head in a fight for survival.

Palace had appointed the flamboyant Malcolm Allison, and let him spend plenty of money. Despite the fact that Ron Saunders had begun to dismantle the promotion-winning side, they still had character in abundance. In my mind our players were heroes: Forbes, Stringer, Keelan, Livermore and the rest, and despite all our troubles, in my heart of hearts I thought they were unbeatable.

City had to win. Palace's superior goal difference meant that a win for them, or a draw, would save them and relegate us. A City win, though, would mean relegation for Palace and almost certain safety for us.

The day of the game was an emotional rollercoaster for me. 'Look East' were at the Post House to see Allison and his Palace team arrive. Allison's easy confidence petrified me – how could the country's leading manager be wrong? When my dad came home, he said that he'd been at the Post House and that, off camera, Allison looked terrified. I didn't know what to think.

The game started disastrously for City: a penalty was awarded against Big Dunc for a 'foul' on Don Rogers. Was it a foul or not? Was it in the area or not? The referee gave it, but the linesman – who was better placed – didn't. Rogers, one of Allison's big-money signings, scored from the penalty spot. The unfairness of it was too much for me, and I broke down.

Fortunately, City were made of much sterner stuff than me – they took control of the game and equalised more or less immediately. The rest of the game followed a pattern that has become so familiar over the years – we dominated but couldn't score. As time ran out it seemed that everything that had preceded the game – the championship win, the heroics against Chelsea and West Brom – was going to be for nothing. City were going to be relegated at the first attempt.

Then we won a corner on the right. Briggs took the kick, Dave Stringer rose to head… and scored! Nothing mattered any more – the run of defeats, the loss at Wembley, the Rogers penalty – all swept away in a moment of pure bliss. I broke down again, but this time they were tears of joy. Take a look at the famous picture of Dave celebrating just after he scored – he looks how I felt.

That was it. There was no time for Palace to come back and we had saved ourselves. I count myself fortunate to have been there. Most people will never have the experience of total despair being turned into undiluted joy in the twinkling of an eye. If there's any justice at all, the new south stand should be called the Dave Stringer Stand or, better still, the Forbes and Stringer Stand.

34

A dramatic night

Manchester United 2–2 Norwich City ☾ League Cup semi-final, first leg ☾ 15 January 1975

By Angus George

Angus George, a Local Government Officer from Great Yarmouth, has earned the right to be dubbed a Norwich City super-fan, having completed a run of over 1000 consecutive games between May 1978 and October 2001.

I have only recently interrupted a sequence of approximately 1000 consecutive games, therefore have a host of memories to call upon. As a regular travel steward on Club Canary, I have supported the club avidly since the early 1960s, so can choose my most memorable match from a period of nearly forty years. My selection is the League Cup semi-final first leg at Old Trafford, played on 15 January 1975.

There were over 58,000 people inside Old Trafford that night, and the noise they generated was unbelievable. I have never experienced anything like it before or since, not even at Wembley.

The drama of the game itself matched that incredible atmosphere. The final scoreline was two-two, but for the vast majority of the ninety minutes Norwich were pinned back inside their own half. Lou Macari opened the scoring for United in the first half and it could easily have been two-nil, but for a tremendous goal-line clearance by John Benson that saved the day. A shot went past Kevin Keelan but seemed to get held up in the heavy mud, and Benson somehow got back to scramble the ball away, wrapping himself around a goalpost in the process. Then, completely against the run of play, Tony Powell equalised for us just on the stroke of half-time.

The second half was definitely one-way traffic towards the goal. United were kicking towards where I was standing at the Scoreboard End, and it seemed as if there was a tidal wave of red shirts coming at us incessantly. A combination of luck and desperate defence helped restrict United to just one second-half goal, Lou Macari scoring his second of the match.

I was reasonably happy to settle for a two-one defeat, so when Ted MacDougall equalised at the Stretford End in the last minute it was a real bonus. The goal came as a result of a complete mix-up in the United defence, and was a virtual carbon copy of Gordon Bolland's winner for City in the FA Cup at Old Trafford in 1967.

The terrific atmosphere, the late equaliser and the whole drama of the occasion are what make this game so memorable for me.

Angus receives a silver salver from then Club Chairman Barry Lockwood in recognition of his loyal support of the Canaries

35

Off to Wembley

Norwich City 1–0 Manchester United ⚽ League Cup semi-final, second leg ⚽ 22 January 1975

By John Bond

John Bond's reign as Norwich City manager lasted seven years between 1973 and 1980 and during that period the Canaries were transformed from a solid, workmanlike outfit to a team with a reputation for playing attractive and entertaining football.

When asked to select my most memorable match from these seven years, I recall a couple of games that would figure highly on anyone's list from that particular period.

Our win over Manchester United in the second leg of the League Cup semi-final at Carrow Road in 1975 is probably the most memorable. Football has changed so much since then, there is so much more money in the game for clubs such as Norwich. In those days it meant so much to the club to be involved in such big games, both financially and in terms of football success.

I said at the time that Ted MacDougall's late equaliser at Old Trafford in the first leg was probably the most significant goal he had ever scored, and I was proved right. The second leg was a tremendous occasion in front of a noisy full house at Carrow Road. Colin Suggett scored the winner and Kevin Keelan played magnificently for me.

As manager of Norwich, over the years I became used to losing, or at best drawing, against Ipswich. I remember feeling that after Ipswich had drawn at Carrow Road in the quarter-finals they thought they were certain to beat us in the replay, and that made our two-one victory at Portman Road even sweeter. Two goals from Johnny Miller, who I signed from Ipswich, took us through to face Manchester United in the semi-final.

City's exhilarating three-two home win over Queen's Park Rangers in April 1976, a result that eventually denied Rangers the championship, would also be on my list, as would a match against Arsenal in January 1977. I have good memories of clashes with Arsenal, both as a player and a manager. On this occasion it was not the game that sticks out for me (Arsenal won one-nil). I had just signed Kevin Reeves on loan from Bournemouth and I stuck him in against Arsenal at Highbury. He was so out of his depth that I was forced to take him off. I can remember people at the Club wondering what the heck I was doing with him. The rest is history: I signed Kevin for £50,000 and sold him three years later for £1 million.

John was back at Carrow Road for the Centenary match with Harwich & Parkeston in September 2002

36

There's always next year

Norwich City 2–3 York City ☙ Second Division ☙ 18 January 1975

By Lee Shepherd

Following the fortunes of the Canaries has been a roller-coaster affair for Lee Shepherd since watching his first game in January 1975.

I was 'initiated' at Carrow Road on the 18th January 1975, aged twelve, on my Dad's shoulders in what felt like a packed River End terrace. (I don't know what the actual attendance that day was.) John Bond had got us playing some good, attractive attacking football and City were heading for promotion back to the old First Division. I had been crazing Dad to let me go to a game for ages – Mum just warned, 'They'll lift you up and then let you down, they always do!'

Well, one Saturday lunchtime, Dad finally succumbed, and on a crisp winter's afternoon, there we were, running over Carrow Bridge unsuccessfully trying to get through the turnstiles before the kick-off. I remember vividly staring at the floodlights as we struggled to get into the ground, and because we were late and I was small for my age, I could see nothing of the game. Just as we reached the top of the steps at the back of the terrace a strange groan came from the crowd – the visitors, York City, had scored! Then, as I tried to come to terms with what was going on around me, with Dad crouching to let me get onto his shoulders, things got worse! Two down to York City (who, as I recall, were Second Division strugglers that season), at home, in ninety seconds! Maybe Mum had got things the wrong way round?

My father was a City supporter all his life, and had been a useful player himself at local league level in North Norfolk. Although I didn't quite have to recite the '59 Cup side every morning before breakfast, let's just say that long before seeing the Canaries in the flesh, I knew that Brennan had scored a perfectly good 'goal' versus Luton in the first game in the semi; and that replaying the tie on a Wednesday afternoon in Birmingham had denied Dad and many others the chance to salute their heroes' valiant, but ultimately vain, attempt to reach Wembley!

Although my first game at Carrow Road was a memorable experience, it's not quite my most treasured Canary moment. That came about three years later, as City tumbled out of the FA Cup at home to that season's giant-killers, Leyton Orient. (Actually they may have been going through one of their periodic name changes and been just plain Orient, but whatever they were called they went all the way to the semi-final before losing to Arsenal, the eventual runners-up.) Orient won 1-0 with a

The programme from the Canaries' clash with York City in 1974/75

Peter Kitchen goal, and I sat there sobbing quietly long after the final whistle.

Dad and I had season tickets in the old Main Stand by now and we were to sit there together for about another three seasons. Later, I would get teenage angst and the urge to get scared witless in the Barclay, but all that lay ahead, and with Dad's comforting arm around me, my distress at City's shameful cup exit was there for all to see. It must have touched the heart of the old boy who edged past us and muttered cheerfully, 'Never mind son, there's always next year!' Even today, some twenty-four years on, I can still see the shock on the older man's face as my Dad looked up and sadly shook his head. 'Always next year, next year! Don't be so bloody stupid man!'

Dad died a couple of years ago and I hope he'll forgive me retelling this story publicly. I know it doesn't show him in a particularly good light. The truth is that he was a wonderfully committed, if occasionally misguided (like all of us) fan of City. He believed in all the good things in the game and deplored all that was bad, hence his distress the afternoon some Manchester United 'supporters' showed their allegiance by trying to demolish the Barclay. So if that elderly man who was on the sharp end of my father's 'enthusiasm' that evening is still around, may I apologise on his behalf,. Despite trips to Villa Park and Hillsborough (and other earlier exits) I'm still waiting for 'next year' as far as City and the FA Cup are concerned.

Oh and one more thing – City fought back but lost two-three to York City that cold January afternoon, it's been a rollercoaster ever since – perhaps my mother was on to something after all. Not that I would have it any other way.

37

Bond and Peters

Norwich City 3–0 Nottingham Forest ◔ Second Division ◔ 19 April 1975

By Peter Meades

Peter, Public Relations Manager for Anglia Railways, is a well-known figure at Norwich City. The first match he attended at Carrow Road was a 1–0 home victory over Bolton Wanderers on 29 October 1966.

Any supporter of Norwich City in the 1970s could rightly claim that this was the decade when the Canaries finally began to shake off their 'country cousins' tag and emerge from the shadow of their more glamorous neighbours down the A140.

Four men were responsible for the progress: visionary chairmen Geoffrey Watling and Sir Arthur South, and Ron Saunders and John Bond in the manager's seat. What a contrast between the two pairs, Watling and Saunders, and then

Phil Boyer notched a brace as City overcame Forest 3–0 in April 1975

South and Bond – both were marriages almost made in heaven.

Bondy was without a doubt the main star. Magic in fact. What a manager, what a character. Larger than life, and always opinionated, you either loved him or hated him. But it was John Bond, indisputably, who shaped the Canaries into a modern-day football club capable of competing with the best.

At his managerial prime, which was probably from 1975 to 1979, it was Bond's ability to sign players who seemed to be either past their best or just underperforming that helped turn City into one of the most entertaining sides in the country. It was not an easy ride for the club, the staff, nor the supporters, as Bondy wore his heart on his sleeve. But the quality of the football was sublime at times – probably the best seen at Carrow Road, with the exception of the 1958/59 cup run and the all-too-brief periods of Dave Stringer and Mike Walker's reign when the club could and perhaps should have won some silverware.

But back to 1974/75. City had been relegated from the old First Division the season before. Bond had reshaped the squad, largely by bringing a legion of players from his old club, Bournemouth – it was rumoured at one stage that City were about to change their colours to red and black. The team lacked consistency, but were always there or thereabouts in the top six of a league that had recently changed to three up, three down. How City were to exploit that, and would do so again in 1981/82!

Just before the transfer deadline in March, Bond swooped to sign the greatest player ever to wear a Canary shirt – World Cup winner Martin Peters, for a bargain £50,000. I can remember the disbelief when I heard the news, and I literally sprinted home to shout down the hall to Mum that City had signed Martin Peters! Now we were going places.

At the time, however, the signing was ridiculed by some of the media, who saw the ex-Spurs and West Ham man as finished. It was true that Peters had not had a happy time towards the end of his White Hart Lane career, booed at times by the fickle Tottenham fans. But Bondy had sold the club to Martin, and how he would repay the faith of his former team-mate (they had both played at West Ham at the beginning of Peters' career there).

Just eight games into his Norwich career, City and Martin Peters faced a struggling Forest team under Brian Clough in the penultimate home game of the season. If City were to maintain their late push for promotion, two points were vital. John Bond's masterstroke was to play Colin Suggett wide on the right, with

Peters released into a free role in central midfield, ably supported by the workaholic Mick McGuire. The formation put him in the ideal position for the late, ghosting runs into the penalty area from which he scored most of his goals. He did just that on this bright, sunny afternoon, producing a typical Peters goal. The quicksilver Phil Boyer – an ideal foil for 'SuperMacDougall' as the crowd sang – popped up with a double, and Forest were brushed aside three-nil. This fine home win set City up for their final away game the following Saturday at Fratton Park, where Peters scored again to help secure promotion back to Division One at the first attempt.

I feel very privileged to have witnessed Martin Peters play for Norwich City. In my opinion he remains the finest and most skilful player ever to have pulled on a yellow shirt, and was also a great ambassador for his club and his profession. Thanks, Martin, for all the pleasure you gave thousands of City fans in the seventies – and thanks also to Bondy!

This is Lee's second great memory from his time as a Norwich City fan.

Just a game?

Norwich City 2–1 Manchester United ⚽ First Division ⚽ 2 April 1977

By Lee Shepherd

Watching the media coverage as the Cardiff versus Leeds United cup tie made headline news during the 2001/02 season, I wondered how many other football supporters' minds were cast back to the dark days of regular hooliganism, during the seventies and eighties.

It may be hard to believe nowadays but pitch invasions, running battles between rival sets of 'fans', and planned violence by groups like the notorious Inter-city Firm were then the norm. Particularly so, I would say, in the ten-year period between 1975 and 1985, culminating in the pitched battle at Kenilworth Road that ended with mainly Millwall 'supporters' hurling ripped up seats at Luton followers, the police, and just about anybody else in the local vicinity. The disturbance led to calls for identity cards and bans on travelling supporters.

Manchester United have long been one of this land's leading football clubs, and on the field they have earned their reputation as one of the greatest football clubs in the world. They have often achieved notable firsts – the first English club to win the European Cup, the first to achieve the much-vaunted treble, and the first club (I think) to be managed by two knights of the realm (Busby and

Ferguson). In the early seventies they also set another, rather less glorious first, when they became the first English club to cage in their own fans!

If you currently dislike Manchester United because they seem to win almost everything and most of their fans appear to live in Basingstoke, other football supporters' reasons for shunning United thirty years ago were entirely different. The Red Devils came to be disliked in many quarters because of a vociferous and unruly element in their support that were apparently hell-bent on causing trouble wherever they went. This hooligan malaise may have had its origins in the pitch invasion at the end of the 1973/74 season, when former idol Denis Law's back-heel consigned United to the Second Division (they came straight back up as champions along with Villa and City). It soon spread throughout the English game. Indeed, the national team was just as likely to be eliminated from major tournaments by some fans' behaviour as by performances on the pitch.

Without resorting to the rural stereotype of Norfolk as a sleepy backwater, it's pretty fair to say that most of the violence growing within the game in the mid-seventies had passed by Norwich City FC and their supporters. Granted, things in the Barclay could occasionally get a bit rough in the years that followed, but by the time Manchester United came to visit in April 1977, the nearest that Carrow Road had got to hooliganism was cushions being hurled on to the pitch by disgruntled patrons in the old Main Stand!

On Saturday 2 April all that changed, irredeemably, forever. In one afternoon large numbers of visiting United supporters went on the rampage, tearing down large sections of the Barclay Stand, overturning cars in the streets around Carrow Road, and terrifying many Norwich fans, and probably some of their own as well. Why? Well, who really knows, but possibly the trigger had been that those upstarts from Norfolk had had the temerity to beat United by two goals to one.

This book is about memories, and I have never forgotten that afternoon. As a slightly naïve fourteen-year-old, genuinely in love with the beautiful game, I had many illusions shattered that day, and I don't mind admitting that I was absolutely terrified. I had never seen violence on that scale before (and haven't since, thankfully) and I have two abiding recollections that have little do to with the football that took place. In fact, I remember little of the game at all – I think Kevin Reeves may have scored the winner – but I was vividly aware of the simmering atmosphere of violence and hate that grew throughout the game.

So much so that I think my eyes were gradually drawn away from the pitch towards the dramatic events unfolding in the Barclay. Writing this, I can almost hear the deafening sound of the splintering wood as United supporters kicked

The programme from the Red Devils' visit to Carrow Road in 1976/77

out large wooden panels at the back of the stand and tore at the inadequate wire mesh fencing separating them from the Norwich fans. At the height of the riot, I remember a United supporter clambering on to the roof of the Barclay while my father (a builder!) speculated that the asbestos roofing would not hold his weight. He was right too, and I watched in horror as the fan fell through the roof and some forty feet on to the concrete terracing below. My other lasting recollection is of watching the police come out of the ground at the end of the match, their uniforms covered from head to foot in spittle – the United fans had vented their anger upon them.

At that time I was a regular autograph hunter at the players' entrance after games. I have happy memories of going on to the Liverpool coach after a match and getting the autographs of most of their 1977 European Cup-winning side. I probably didn't feel much like collecting autographs following the United game, but I guess my Dad probably wanted to try and console me by getting something positive from the afternoon. He knew that, like many young lads, I had secretly always had a soft spot for Manchester United (he himself had told me that as a twenty-year-old he had shed tears for the United players lost at Munich).

As I look today at the signatures of great players like Martin Buchan, and less well-remembered ones like Alex Forsythe, it is hard to recall just how desolate I felt that day, but as if to round things off the occasion was to have one further bitter twist. Just before the United players' coach departed, Tommy Docherty emerged hastily to clamber on board. My Dad pushed me forward to ask for his autograph and I duly held out my treasured book with baited breath. Now, I guess 'the Doc' had probably had rather a trying afternoon, what with the defeat, and I seem to recall United supporters ignoring the plaintive appeals for calm he'd made out on the pitch. He was clearly in no mood to oblige me or any other eager autograph hunters, and my afternoon of misery was completed as he roughly barged me out of the way and disappeared on to the United bus.

Had my Dad had the legs, I am convinced that he would have pursued the bus all the way back to Old Trafford, as it was I remember him chasing it almost all the way to Carrow Bridge! In a peculiar way, I am very grateful to Dad for that, because it's a nice memory – the only nice memory of a truly dreadful afternoon.

39

Twenty missing years

By David Tubby

David, whose favourite moment
is recalled on page 20,
remembers the joys of following
his favourite team before the
hooliganism of the mid 1970s
led to a 20-year sabbatical.

I wonder how many City fans in their mid-fifties missed most of the First Division years. I stopped watching at the height of football hooliganism in 1977 – remember Manchester United and the Barclay Stand? I returned in 1997, at a time when we needed all the support we could get, and became a season ticket holder in 1998.

OK, so I went to a handful of matches during those years, but I missed a winning return to Wembley, a famous European campaign, Fashanu, Woods, Watson, Bruce, Deehan, Gordon, Crook, Fox, Sutton (I saw his dad) and most of Gunn… sorry Bryan!

I saw my first match at Carrow Road in about 1956, when City played QPR in the old Third Division South. I can recall the blue and white hooped shirts of the opposition, and that Reg Foulkes played a good part of the match with blood pouring from a cut forehead. I stood near the front railings roughly where the away fans sit today.

I haven't tracked down the exact date of that first match, but my second was on 28 September 1957, against Bournemouth. A coach owned by Bensleys of Martham picked up my granddad and me in Clippesby. I remember someone on the coach conducting a raffle by selling discs with different scores on. We stood on the open terracing at the River End, City drew two-two, and I have vague memories of Ken Oxford in goal and a blond wing-half called Bobby Wilson.

I may have missed a lot during those heady First Division years, but from 1957 to 1977 we also had a few highlights: the 1959 cup run, 1959–60 promotion, 1962 League Cup, the 1971/72 promotion and two losing Wembley League Cup Finals. I still have the programmes for the games against Rochdale (home), Spurs and Aston Villa, and yes, I missed the win over Sunderland in '85.

There were a few grim years of Division Two survival in the sixties, but those twenty years also gave City fans plenty to shout about, starting of course with the '59ers. I was only able to go to two of the games, but what a duo – Manchester United in the snow and Tottenham Hotspur under floodlights. Memories revolve around the long winding queues for tickets on Sunday mornings, the tightly packed crowds, particularly at the Tottenham game, and Terry Bly. Terry became a hero when he scored the winner against Spurs, while being marked by the former City centre-half and England international Monty Norman.

I may have had the privilege of attending only two games of that cup run, but I can vividly recall sitting in front of the fire at our Caister smallholding listening to the radio commentary of the Sheffield United reply, and the semi-final draw with Luton at White Hart Lane. My dad had gone to the latter match while suffering with 'flu, and I still have the programme he brought me home. School intervened to prevent any close monitoring of the Luton replay, which for some reason was played on a midweek afternoon.

My main memory of the 1959/60 promotion season is of the four-three win against Southend. This was the penultimate game of the season and clinched promotion to Division Two. This was one of the few games I watched from the main stand, and my abiding memory was the pace of the victory.

I firmly believed that where you stood in the ground had an influence on who your favourite players were. In those early years I mainly stood halfway up the Barclay, behind the goal. This position favoured goalkeepers and goal-scorers – Kennon, Keelan, Allcock, Davies and Curran. Later on, following the influx of away support, many of us moved for safety reasons to the Barclay end of the new South Stand, and then an affinity with left-backs and right-wingers developed – Black, Benson, Foggo and Briggs. Strangely my two all-time Canary favourites played mainly at left-half: Matt Crowe and his successor in that position, Joe Mullett.

Matt seemed to stroll through a game with so much time on the ball, and Joe was a combative player whose cracking twenty-five-yard goal in a five-nil FA Cup win over Newcastle remains in my memory. By the way, a certain Terry Allcock scored the other four that night.

I have two prominent memories of that first season in Division Two, which was played in front of home crowds that regularly exceeded 20,000, and occasionally 30,000.

The first was Terry Allcock's broken leg against Plymouth Argyle on a sunny late summer evening in early September 1960. Terry was playing in front of his Norfolk Minor County cricket colleagues, who were then playing Lancashire Second XI in the

Challenge match for the Minor Counties title. It was the first time that I had witnessed such a serious injury.

The second, more pleasant memory occurred later that same month in a game against Lincoln City that Norwich won five-one. Jimmy Hill struck a shot from just outside the penalty area that hit the bar, rebounded, and Jimmy rose to head the ball back into the net. At least I was convinced that happened in this match, until I recently looked up the match report in the back copies of the EDP. According to the report this was one of Jimmy's more magical performances and he scored two goals, but neither was described as I imagined. So much for memories; I must have got the wrong match.

It's strange how little I can remember of the 1971/72 promotion season. I have vague visions of those resolute defenders Forbes and Stringer, and Keelan's acrobatics; this perhaps personified Saunders' team, built on fitness and sound defence.

Third time lucky at Wembley in 1985

City's first Division One goal, scored by Jimmy Bone, must be remembered by all of us who were there. To me, however, the most memorable goal of that first season in the top grade was a Graham Paddon free-kick against Stoke City. Taken from several yards outside the penalty area at the Barclay End, it simply screamed into the net.

I am writing this shortly after a nil-nil FA Cup draw with Chelsea, so it is with Chelsea that I will finish. Those who attended will never forget the anguish we all suffered leading up to the eventual abandonment of the famous League Cup Second Leg semi-final in 1973. I stood in the Barclay End of the South Stand and had no idea what was happening beyond the River End penalty area. Then the far side of the pitch under the Main Stand became obscured, and the rest is history. The relief we all felt when Steve Govier's headed goal in the rearranged match sealed a first ever trip to Wembley was immense.

I am now five seasons into what will hopefully be at least another twenty years of Carrow Road action. Who knows, 2002 could just be the turning point. Just as Ron Saunders turned round the mediocrity of the Lol Morgan years, let us hope that Nigel Worthington can continue to revitalise the Canaries.

40

Why Norwich?

Leeds United 2–2 Norwich City ◯ First Division ◯ 5 November 1977

By Robert Gray

A chance encounter on returning from a family holiday has led to a 30-year odyssey for Yorkshire lad Robert. He didn't even have to watch a match to become a fan, the sight of thousands of yellow-and-green bedecked supporters outside Carrow Road was enough to convince him that Norwich City was the team for him. His first match, a heavy FA Cup defeat at Leeds, did nothing to dampen his considerable enthusiasm.

'Why Norwich?' It's a question I've heard constantly over the last thirty years while following my beloved club. It's hardly surprising though, as I was born in Halifax, West Yorkshire, in the early 1960s, and have lived there all my life.

I have stood on terrace many times with the other Canary faithful, only to receive puzzled looks because of my accent. Obviously 'On the ball, City' doesn't quite sound the same with a Yorkshire twang! People must have thought I was jumping on the bandwagon, so to speak, particularly when the team was doing so well in the old First Division and early Premiership days. Not so! My story goes back to long before Norwich ever played top-flight football.

So, why Norwich? Well, a strange combination of events led to me wearing yellow and green rather than blue and white – no, I don't just mean Ipswich, but Halifax too. It started around my fourth birthday, when I went to stay with an aunt in Blackpool for a holiday. The house was beside Blackpool airport, and from my bedroom I spent hour after hour that week watching the aircraft. Aviation became a fascination of mine, and after starting to build model kits a couple of years later I began to show a real passion for the subject.

My dad started telling me the stories of his wartime years spent on the United States Eighth Air Force bases in East Anglia. Through these tales I learned of many things as a child long before I read them in books as a young man – about the aircraft, the units involved, and details of missions such as the Russian shuttle raids performed by the 100th Bomb Group at Thorpe Abbotts. I also learnt place-names such as Thetford, Beccles, Bungay, Bury St Edmunds and, of course, Norwich, to name but a few. At the age of eight, I'd had an introduction to the East of England – an area that a lot of my schoolmates had never even heard of. The seeds had been sown.

The only sporting interest I had at this stage was in Speedway racing. My brother John followed our local team, the Halifax Dukes, all over the country. These travels included many trips to King's Lynn, who not only raced in the colours of the Canaries but took the nickname 'the stars' from the old Norwich speedway team that had closed at the end of the 1964 season. I still hadn't shown any interest in football and had always looked upon the Shay stadium as a speedway venue, not a football ground.

But at the age of ten, at the start of the 1971/72 football season, we were returning home from a family holiday when Dad drove past Carrow Road on a match day. I remember vividly the masses of yellow and green covering the terracing of the old Barclay end. This left an enormous impression, so much so that I followed City's results that season, though I didn't quite declare myself a supporter just yet. Of course the Canaries won the League, and I decided to keep my eye on them for another year. Their first trip to Wembley followed, and needless to say after these two events I decided to become a true supporter of the club.

That's when it all went horribly wrong – relegation! But I wasn't too bothered – Norwich were my team now, and although I didn't know it at the time, we were going to enjoy some special times together. The halcyon days of that 1974/75 season were simply magic, with promotion and Wembley again. Many of my true heroes were included in those mid-seventies teams: McDougall, Boyer, Keelan, Forbes and the great Martin Peters. Is it really all those years ago?

There were many ups and downs though, even then. In 1975/76 wins at Liverpool and Leeds, two of the best teams at that time, were followed by a typical cup defeat at home to Bradford City, a team in a re-election place (bottom of the Fourth Division). Did I get some stick at school over that one! My English teacher was a Bradford fan and as I was the only one in school with a yellow and green scarf on, he could see me coming a mile off.

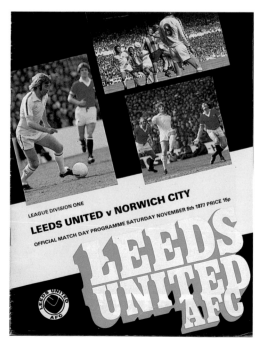

The programme for City's visit to Elland Road in 1977

The first time I saw Norwich live, my Dad took me to Leeds to see the FA Cup mauling in 1977. Five-one down at half time – I copped it again at school. It would have been enough to put anyone off, but not me – after all, I'd just seen Martin Peters score! It was a job convincing my Dad to take me to another match, but he eventually relented and we returned to Elland Road the following November. I am so glad we did – what a match.

We were leading two-one at half-time with goals from John Ryan and Roger Gibbins. Leeds equalised very early in the second half, and from that moment on the Canaries were pinned back in their own half. Shots rained on the Norwich goal, but Kevin Keelan performed heroics in a display I have yet to see surpassed. All in front of the Geldered end too, it didn't come much better than that. It was just a great shame that matches in those days didn't have the same TV coverage as today – a lot of

1977

Norwich fans would not have seen that display. I wasn't a bit surprised when Kevin was voted above Peter Shilton of Nottingham Forest as Division One goalkeeper of the season. Surely the best goalkeeper never to play for England, for me – only Bryan Gunn has come close to emulating the great man.

I've enjoyed following the Canaries and I am proud and as passionate about my club as anyone in Norfolk. I dread to think of the outcome if Dad had driven down Portman Road instead of Carrow Road all those years ago – it sends shivers down the spine!

41

Denied at the death

Coventry City 5–4 Norwich City ● First Division ● 27 December 1977

By Richard Futter

Local journalist and broadcaster Richard Futter admits to having been a Canaries fan since the mid-1960s, when Welsh international striker Ron Davies was his hero and Norwich City were only an average Second Division outfit.

I remember reporting on the Canaries when John Bond was manager. He was always so open; nothing was kept secret, even transfer stories were shared. Local journalists were sometimes invited to pre-match team talks and post-match inquests, which could be very embarrassing.

For my most memorable match I look back to Coventry away at the end of 1977. As a football reporter I normally worked in tandem with my colleague Mick Dennis, but for this particular match over the Christmas holiday he stayed at home, leaving me to file two separate reports on my own for the first time. This game ended in a five-four win for Coventry City with enough incidents to keep a team of journalists busy, never mind a relatively inexperienced one working on his own for the first time.

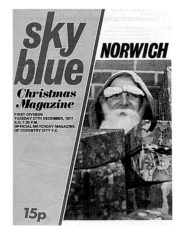

The programme from the nine-goal thriller at Highfield Road in December 1977

The goals were flying in all over the place, and to compound my difficulties it was as cold that day as I can ever remember it being when I was reporting on a match. The ink in each of my three pens froze, so I could hardly scribble any notes. It is just as well that there was plenty of action, otherwise I think we would have all frozen solid.

The game ebbed and flowed with the Canaries leading three-two at half-time before finding themselves five-four behind in the closing minutes, having been awarded a penalty kick. I remember John Ryan's spot-kick, after he had already scored from one, being saved by Jim Blyth, denying Norwich a well-deserved point.

42

A classic Canary goal

Norwich City 3–5 Liverpool ☙ First Division ☙ 9 February 1980

By Roy Waller

Roy here gets the opportunity to recall another memorable moment from the 1979/80 season.

I had the pleasure of taking my son Paul to the Norwich City–Liverpool game at Carrow Road that starred the late Justin Fashanu.

It was a very exciting match that Liverpool dominated, with David Fairclough scoring a hat-trick, but the goal of the game was when Justin picked up the ball, strode forward, and struck a tremendous shot high into the roof of the net. It turned out to be the BBC's Goal of the Season and is still shown on television.

Despite this stunning goal I was very upset that Liverpool went on to win the game with ease. When the final Liverpool goal went in I grabbed my son and left the ground before the end, despite his objections. I was so disgusted by the Norwich performance that I stunned my friends around me by leaving without a word.

The goal has remained in my memory since then and my son often reminds me that he was deprived of seeing the last minutes of a very good game, despite the final score. It's ironic that as a commentator now on all Norwich City matches I have no excuse for leaving a game just because the Canaries are playing badly!

Justin Fashanu attempting the spectacular against Liverpool

43

A vital match

Leicester City 1–4 Norwich City ◌ Second Division ◌ 1 May 1982

By Malcolm Robertson

Malcolm Robertson reported on the fortunes of Norwich City between the years of 1978 and 1985 as a journalist with Eastern Counties Newspapers and then, between 1985 and 1990, as Sports Producer of BBC Radio Norfolk.

When asked to select my most memorable match I cast my mind back to when the Canaries produced a tremendous display to beat promotion rivals Leicester City at Filbert Street.

It was a vital match. We were in the middle of a fantastic run of eleven wins in twelve matches, and Leicester were probably our closest rivals for the third promotion place.

To say we crushed them would be an understatement. After Eddie Kelly hit our post early on, we ruthlessly swept aside their challenge. John Deehan put us one-nil ahead before half-time, taking advantage of a poor Mark Wallington goal kick, but our second-half performance was as good as anything I can remember. We scored three goals quite early in the half through Mark Barham, Keith Bertschin and a spectacular own-goal from Norman Leet.

Although Larry May scored a last-minute consolation goal, this single victory really turned optimistic hopes of promotion into a real possibility.

It was a remarkable final third of the season that took us from about fourteenth position in late February to clinching promotion at Hillsborough in mid-May. The arrival of Martin O'Neill in February acted as a catalyst for this exciting run, instilling a real sense of self-belief amongst players and supporters alike.

Mark Barham who took part in the Centenary match was on target in City's 4–1 win at Filbert Street in 1982

The Pink Un recalls City's 4–1 win at Filbert Street

EASTERN Football News

Saturday May 1st 1982

(THE PINK UN)

No. 2081—14p Tel. 28311

We stock a wide range of REGIMENTALITIES and CUFF LINKS; BADGES available on special order

CHADDS 21 BEDFORD STREET, NORWICH 22688

ADIDAS BADMINTON £9.

INSIDE PAGES Hoveton happy —2 | Grove's title — 3 | Soapbox — 4 / City Page —5 | Hope for Loke — 6 | Hughes blow — 7

LOWESTOFT CUP TRIUM

Zino and Freddie have the last laugh

Talk of terraces

● LINDA CURL, who was on target: '88 Lowestoft Waves won the WFA Cup Final for the first time today.

FOUR–GOAL CITY HAVE LEICESTER GASP NG

VERDICT

44

Promotion anxiety

Sheffield Wednesday 2–1 Norwich City ☾ Second Division ☾ 15 May 1982

By Mike Burt

Long-time supporter Mike Burt attended his first match on New Year's Eve 1966. The 3–3 draw with Birmingham City was more than enough to make a fan of Mike, who here describes the agony and the ecstasy of the nail-biting final match of the season at Hillsborough. Norwich may have lost the match, but they won promotion to the First Division.

As matches go this was certainly no classic, but its highs and lows made this my most memorable game in thirty-five years of following the Canaries! I was among the thousands of fans at Hillsborough who suffered the gut-wrenching anxiety of waiting to find out if we had achieved our goal and returned to the promised land of the First Division at the first attempt.

Our status amongst the elite of English football had been lost the previous May, when a three-two home defeat at the hands of already-doomed Leicester City had signalled the end of a brave fight for survival. Strangely, it was the result of Leicester City's match with Shrewsbury that was the focus of Canary anxiety that May afternoon.

A point would almost certainly have been enough to secure promotion. This followed a run of ten wins out of eleven games that had catapulted the Canaries from mid-table obscurity to the brink of promotion in nine weeks. The key factors that sparked this amazing run were the signings of John Deehan and Martin O'Neill in January and February of 1982.

Canaries' Lotteries Manager Mike Burt recalls sealing promotion at Hillsborough as his most memorable match

Back to the match itself. As always, the thousands of travelling fans were offering their team great support. The first half was uninspiring, with few chances at either end and no goals. The home side took the lead early in the second half to put Canary supporters' hearts firmly in their mouths. Then came the moment of joyous celebration as Keith Bertschin equalised (I never agreed with those who compared him to a headless chicken). But with one foot in the First Division, and the minutes ticking away, disaster struck when Sheffield Wednesday again took the lead, leaving thousands believing that the dream was turning to a nightmare.

With time rapidly running out, we desparately needed news of Leicester City's progress against Shrewsbury. Rumours that they were leading swept round the visiting supporters, and when the final whistle sounded many believed that the dream of promotion was dead. Then – joy of joys – the news came through that Leicester had in fact drawn nil-nil and could no longer overhaul City's points total.

Promotion was secure – but what an emotional rollercoaster we had endured.

Before the 1981/82 season, it had been decided that teams would receive three points for a win rather than two. This meant that Norwich finished the season one point ahead of Sheffield Wednesday and were consequently promoted, whereas under the old system we would have finished a point behind them and remained in the Second Division. It's a funny old game!

45

Going up

Sheffield Wednesday 2–1 Norwich City ⚽ Second Division ⚽ 15 May 1982

By Keith Bertschin

Thirty-eight goals in 138 games for the Canaries endeared Keith Bertschin to the Carrow Road faithful. He was a tremendously enthusiastic frontrunner whose non-stop, all-action style made him a real handful for any defence. Signed in August 1981, he was a virtual ever-present in the City team until he left to join Stoke City in November 1984.

I look back to the first season at Carrow Road for my most memorable match. As I remember it we went into the final game of the season at Hillsborough needing a point to be certain of promotion. We were on a great run, having lost just one game since the middle of March, coming from nowhere to within a hair's breadth of promotion.

We went one-nil behind and there was a lot of tension out there on the pitch. With about two minutes of the match to go I headed in an equaliser, which we, and the thousands of fans at the game, thought would guarantee promotion.

As it happened, Wednesday immediately went up the other end to make it two-one. We were all totally confused, there was someone on the pitch as they scored and we just did not know what was happening. First we were struggling, then we thought we were up and then we were out again.

A few minutes after the final whistle we found out that Leicester, who were the only team who could catch us, had only drawn, which meant we were up. We all felt a bit flat after losing our game, but the infectious enthusiasm and excitement of Reserve striker John Fashanu soon spread through the team as we realised what we had achieved.

Keith was on target for the Canaries on the final day of the '81/'82 campaign

46

Derby delight

Ipswich Town 2–3 Norwich City ⚽ First Division ⚽ 27 December 1982

By Peter Mendham

Peter Mendham played a total of 262 senior games for the Club between 1978 and 1996. He was a member of two sides which gained promotion from the Second Division and also the Milk Cup-winning team of 1985.

A stand-out memory for me is the defeat of Ipswich at Portman Road just after Christmas in 1982. The Canaries were in a poor run of form whilst Ipswich were battling away nearer the top of the table. I had been out of the side for some time, and I did not expect to play, but as we got off the coach Ken Brown told me I was playing in place of skipper Mick McGuire. Another new face in the Norwich side that day was former England striker Mick Channon, who was about to embark upon a very successful late chapter in his career.

Another reason for this particular game sticking out in my memory was that my future wife Gabby and step-brother Craig were there to see the game, and it was the first time they had seen me play.

I recall Mark Barham, who was also recalled to the team, setting me up for the first goal. It was such a good cross that I only had to put my head to the ball to score. As a midfield player I had always felt that scoring goals was an important part of my game, and this one really helped me settle into the match.

Ipswich equalised just before half-time through Russell Osman.

My second goal was one of those 'hit and hope' volleys. I knew as soon as I hit it that it was a perfect strike. The ball hit the underside of the crossbar and for a split second I wasn't sure if it had gone in or not, but it bounced into the roof of the net. I remembered running to Gabby to celebrate.

Action from the Canaries' 3–2 win at Portman Road on Boxing Day 1982

Once again Ipswich pulled themselves level, but it was Norwich City who had the final say in this fiercely contested local derby.

I would have loved to have got a hat-trick but I never had a chance. It was

Martin O' Neill who scored the winner with a fantastic direct free-kick in the last minute, and although Alan Brazil nearly equalised again in injury time, we hung on for a deserved victory.

It was a great feeling after the game, meeting up with Gabby and Craig. One thing that did upset me a little bit was the way the media gave all the praise to Martin's winner rather than my contribution, but that was insignificant compared to the memory of a great day.

47

Hope against hope

Liverpool 0–2 Norwich City ☾ First Division ☾ 23 April 1983

By Paul Slater

Paul, an architectural technician, attended his first match at Carrow Road on 15 AprIl 1967, when the Canaries triumphed 4–3 over Crystal Palace in a Second Division fixture. Here he recalls a First Division match that was a high point in a very memorable week for Norwich City.

One of the things that all football supporters have – to varying degrees – is hope. Hope that your boys can defy the odds, that they can continue their rise up the league, and that when they visit the champions-elect the top dogs have an off day.

Having seen their team lose to the footballing might of Brighton, Notts County and Swansea in a very hard first season back in the top flight, it was with a fair amount of hope that three twenty-somethings set off for Merseyside on that bright Spring morning. As those defeats suggest, Norwich were having a poor season and were languishing in the lower reaches of Division One (then the top division). Liverpool, on the other hand, could clinch the Championship – again – this afternoon if Man United lost to Watford and they beat these interlopers from East Anglia.

In the days before the A14 link, a journey north meant plenty of pre-planning, map-reading and the preparation of a Plan B – just in case. However, this trip turned out to be uneventful, and before we knew it we were on the outskirts of the city and following some red-bedecked supporters to a parking space on a side street near Stanley Park.

Inside the ground there was a fair smattering of yellow and green, but at the other end was the awesome sight of a full and flowing Kop – expectant of another major trophy this afternoon. Perhaps diluted by innumerable appearances on TV, the stadium wasn't as impressive as we had been imagining on the journey up. It was still finer than Carrow Road though, and a further difference was the noise that accompanied the players' emergence from the tunnel. Our hopes receded slightly, but as all fans know, hope never dies.

The names on the Liverpool teamsheet were a veritable 'who's who' of international football, but nearly all were from the UK – unlike today. Norwich boasted a few internationals – past, present and future – of their own.

Right from the kick-off the game ebbed and flowed – we mostly ebbed, and the red tide flowed continually towards our penalty area. It was a backs-to-the-wall situation, but our defence formed a formidable barrier, and when it was breached there was further insurance in the form of future England goalkeeper Chris Woods. The Boston boy was to have an immense afternoon. Time and again his reflexes, positioning and instinctive reactions were called upon, and every time they were up to the task in hand. And when it was needed, luck – that essential attribute of successful footballers – came to his rescue, but nobody there that day could deny that he deserved it.

Our hopes got a major boost early in the second half when Mark Barham went down the right flank and crossed the ball to the near stick. To the shock and dismay of the home support, and the delight of us travellers, Mark Lawrenson stuck out a leg and diverted the ball into his own net – one-nil to the Norwich boys!

'Can we hold on to this?' 'I hope so.' Surely not against this all-conquering team. But tell that to Mr Woods. Brilliant before the goal, after it he was beyond belief. Shot after shot, header after header – from every distance and angle – was somehow pushed away from goal. Then, with ten minutes to go, hope gave way to exuberance. Martin O'Neill picked up the ball on the left-hand side of the pitch near the halfway line. He moved forward, unchallenged, and closed in on the penalty area. Then he unleashed an unstoppable thirty-yard rocket into the top left-hand corner of Grobbelaar's net. As he came over to our corner, we shared thirty seconds of pure joy – two-nil to the Canaries!

'Brucie, Brucie, what's the score?' More delight followed as Mr Grobbelaar went into one of his handstand routines to acknowledge that we were two-nil up – great showmanship and entertainment. Our applause for Bruce, though, was nothing compared to the tribute that the Kop afforded Chris Woods at the final whistle. You couldn't hear yourself think, such was the cacophony that rose in appreciation of his display. We had done the double over Liverpool, having won one-nil at Carrow Road earlier in the season, and this was only their fifth defeat of another championship-winning campaign.

Our hopes had been justified – as they are from time to time! Homeward bound and with the Kop anthem on our lips – '…walk on with hope in your heart, and you'll never walk alone' – thoughts turned to Match of the Day. Luckily Andy's dad had taped it and we sat down fairly late to relive our amazing day out. This was the crowning glory – as Martin's shot sailed into the net, the cameras panned to the contingent of City followers, and there in the middle of the throng were three Norfolk boys bouncing up and down in sheer delight. We knew it was us – the one in the middle had a very large, very loud yellow coat on that my sister had got for me!

This game was one of three notable games in a week. We beat Arsenal three-one and drew one-all with Manchester United at Carrow Road either side of this great result at Anfield. As a Norwich fan you always hope that the return of those days is just around the corner.

Martin O'Neill who became City boss in 1995 was on the scored sheet as City won 2–0 at Anfield in 1983

1983

48

A forgotten figure

Norwich City 3–3 Manchester United ◐ First Division ◐ 1 October 1983

By Rob Butcher

Rob, who now lives in Wigan, spent his formative Canary years on the old terrace at the River End. His first match was a Division One home fixture against Liverpool (22 January 1977) with Norwich triumphing 2–1 over the team that went on to win the league that season.

Every City supporter has a favourite spot from which they prefer to watch their heroes. Having defected to the Barclay in the mid-eighties, where I have been ever since, I will always rue the disappearance of the old terrace.

My most formative years were spent swaying in its huge mass of bodies, gesticulating to away fans through the fencing and surging forward on every City goal. But I often cast my mind back to my apprenticeship in the rather more sedate surroundings of the River End, where I learnt the facts of life from my father in the late seventies and formed the friendships that have stayed with me since. And where I developed, even back then, a deep resentment of Manchester United.

On this particular day, my mates and I had taken our usual spot in between the crash barrier and the advertising hoardings. Sporting scarves tied around each wrist and fashionable cloth peaked caps, we were aware of the abundance of United fans around us. This, we would learn, was a regular occurrence when clubs like them and Liverpool played at Carrow Road.

These were the most loyal fans in the world, we would be reminded. They'd always supported them, they'd say. Never even been anywhere near Manchester though, and probably wouldn't even know how to get there. These fans would do anything to get tickets for this match, for they were making their annual trip to watch their heroes from their homes in Great Yarmouth and Lowestoft.

United, they informed us all, were the greatest even then. And on the day in question it looked like they actually had a fair point. Halfway through the second half, they were three-nil up.

Being three down at home to Manchester United was not my idea of a terrific way to spend a Saturday afternoon, even at the age of thirteen. It probably wasn't Mike Pickering's either. But that's exactly what both of us were faced with – I from my usual place in the front row of the River End, and he, a forgotten figure from City folklore, from the sidelines as a second half substitute in what would be his sole City appearance. There was little indication of what was about to happen as the loan signing made his way on to the turf at the home of football itself with some twenty minutes or so left.

And soon afterwards, with numbers in the River End already dwindling and emphasising how much red and black there was in the crowd that day, City pulled a consolation goal back. Just a consolation you understand. That's what the United fans told us anyway.

Dave Bennett, soon to be owner of an Ibizan bar that I would frequent in later life, headed in a far-post cross to muted applause from Canary fans and derisory sarcasm from the Red Devils fans. When I encountered him in Ibiza years later he looked a bit surprised at the adulation and attention to detail with which I relayed his contribution in this game – but he still charged me for my drinks!

OFFICIAL MATCH DAY PROGRAMME
PRICE 50p

CANON LEAGUE DIVISION ONE
**NORWICH CITY
v MANCHESTER UNITED**
Saturday, October 1, 1983
Kick Off 3.00 p.m.

TODAY'S MATCH IS SPONSORED BY
SPRUCE HOWLETT
Norfolk's leading Ford Dealer

*The programme from the thrilling
3–3 draw with Red Devils in 1983*

Then, with a few minutes to go, up popped Mick Channon, ex-England international and once described by Brian Moore as 'the most rampant striker in the world' but now plying his trade with the Canaries. Dispatching Bennett's free kick with a bullet header into the top corner, he wheeled away on one of his infamous goal celebrations, swinging his arm in delight as the City players tried to catch him.

A different mood fell over Carrow Road. Silence had fallen unexpectedly amongst the once-vociferous United fans, whilst there was delight upon the faces of City followers. The noise level trebled as we contemplated the unlikely possibility of unexpectedly snatching something from the jaws of defeat.

And we did. With seconds left on the clock a frantic goalmouth scramble took place, the ball bobbled about a bit, the United defence failed to clear it, and up popped Louie Donowa to score from an almost horizontal position. Which was quite apt for him – most of his performances were so laid back. But who cared. As the ball nestled firmly in the back of the old onion bag, he lay buried under a sea of City players celebrating an unbelievable comeback.

We indulged in a celebration of our own, and attempted to include the United fans in our thoughts, but alas we were too late. For they had already gone. Their loyalty knew bounds after all.

The stony-faced United followers trudged back to Yarmouth with their tails between their legs and their heads hung low. Mike Pickering left the Canaries and drifted off to an obscure and rarely visited corner of City legend. My mates and I shortly moved home to the Barclay Stand, but with us we took the passion that still remains with us, even if we don't tie scarves around our wrist any more.

49

Tormenting the Hornets

Norwich City 6–1 Watford ✪ First Division ✪ 7 April 1984

By John Deehan

John made his debut for Norwich City on 28 December 1981 in a home fixture against Luton Town, scoring one of the 70 goals that made him popular with both team mates and supporters throughout his three-and-a-half-year playing career with the Club. John returned to Carrow Road in the '90s as Assistant Manager and subsequently became Manager following Mike Walker's departure to Everton in January 1994.

John in action as he notches four goals in City's 6–1 romp over the men from Vicarage Road

I managed to score four of the goals when we beat Watford six-one at Carrow Road. Our form leading into the game had been indifferent. We were slipping towards the foot of the table and were therefore under quite a lot of pressure.

My memory of the day's events is crystal clear, and I can recall each of the game's most important moments as if they happened yesterday.

My first goal came as a result of a long clearance from Chris Woods. The ball bounced and it was a fifty-fifty ball between me and Sherwood, the Watford keeper. I got the touch, looped the ball home and was very surprised he didn't knock me into next week.

I scored my second with a very clean, powerful strike after playing a one-two with Mick Channon. We had been working hard on shooting in practice that week and it really paid off.

Greg Downs had made it two-nil between my first two goals and then Mo Johnston pulled one back before half-time to make it three-one.

There was still a chance that we might capitulate. Chris Woods saved a penalty and then we were awarded one when debutant Robert Rosario was fouled. There was a brief thought that we should let Robert take the kick, but the bench were adamant that I should take it. I scored, and soon after we were given another penalty. I took that one too and scored again.

John Devine rounded the victory off superbly with a thundering drive, but it was my four-goal show that stole the headlines: to score four goals in a First Division match was a very rare feat indeed. But my torment of Watford didn't end there – I scored another Carrow Road hat-trick against them the following season!

50

Part of something special

Grimsby 0–1 Norwich City ⚽ Milk Cup fifth round ⚽ 16 January 1985

By Martin Thirkettle

This is Martin's second contribution to this collection of 100 great footballing moments.

This game may not have been a classic, but it highlights the intrepid nature of football supporters who feel that something special is about to happen and that they want to be a part of it.

The weather on that dull, snow-laden January day was bad enough to make Ranulph Fiennes tuck his huskies away, put his feet up in front of a blazing fire and grab the nearest bottle of single malt. Myself, Kevin (my ex-brother in law) and Mike, a work colleague, had arranged to travel to Grimsby on a coach that was scheduled to leave County Hall at two in the afternoon. During the morning, the snow was already settling, and it was announced that there would be a pitch inspection at three o'clock to determine whether the match would go ahead. Throughout the morning phone calls flew back and forth between County Hall and ourselves, and we eventually decided to risk the journey, even though we wouldn't know if the game was on or not until we were at least one hour out of Norwich.

The coach provided some relief from the Arctic conditions. It had a video, and this was in the days when you were allowed to take alcohol on board. As we made our way out of Norfolk, the bleak flatness of the Lincolnshire countryside, which makes even the Acle Straight look hilly, could have passed for Siberia. We eventually heard on the radio that the match was on, just as we pulled in for the inevitable stop at the Farm Shop on the A17.

We arrived in the not-too-sunny resort of Cleethorpes at about six o'clock, the coach parking up on the landward side of the sea wall in Harrington Street, just a stone's throw from the ground in one direction and an icicle's width from the North Sea in the other. Mike, ever the beer connoisseur, had prior knowledge of a nearby real-ale outlet, for which we headed in order to replenish our stocks for the journey home. This done, we went off in search of a suitable pre-match hostelry, while ever-increasing numbers of arriving Norwich fans engaged in friendly snowball fights with the local police.

The next incident was probably one of the oddest that I have ever experienced in all my years of trying to find a decent pre-match pub. We were on the main road running south from the ground when a woman suddenly appeared from a darkened hulk of a building that looked like an empty hotel. From the exterior, there were no signs of life at all, not even a crack of light between the heavy, tightly drawn curtains. Mysteriously, she asked if we were looking for somewhere to drink, then pulled us into the blacked-out building before we had a chance to answer. When the stout door was opened, we were greeted with the sight of hundreds of Norwich fans, merrily drinking and singing their heads off. I looked around the bar and saw many people I recognised, including an old school friend, Dave Perry, who thought that most of Norwich had made the trip to Grimsby despite the appalling weather conditions. In fact, about 5000 Norwich fans had made the journey, in the coldest and most difficult conditions I had ever travelled to an away match in. The feeling in the bar that evening was electric, the anticipation tangible.

Inside the ground, the Norwich fans were packed into the Osmond Stand, behind one of the goals, which was divided into standing at the front and cramped wooden seating at the rear. For some unknown reason we had four-pound seats when all of us would have preferred to stand. We did, however, have a good view of the pitch, although the goalmouth was partially obscured by the perimeter fencing. We also had a good view of all the Norwich fans streaming into the ground, many in fancy dress, including one bloke decked out in a Pink Panther suit from head to foot who spent most of his time climbing up the perimeter fencing, spurring on the Norwich faithful.

The pitch itself was rock-hard, but the snow had been removed, giving a difficult but clear surface. As the match progressed, it became obvious that City were making the best of the conditions. We only had to wait until the twenty-ninth minute for a goal, when John Deehan's near-post header beat Nigel Batch in the Grimsby goal. Celebrations went into overdrive. From then on, and throughout the second half, there was a constant barrage of noise from the City fans, while at the other end Chris Woods was facing an equally constant barrage of snowballs from the home fans who were desperately trying to distract him. The travelling support went ballistic when the final whistle sounded. The trip home would be one to savour, buoyed up by our replenished stocks of alcohol.

The match against Grimsby was one of eight on the road to Wembley

Having said that, one person did not have such a good journey home. We'd been celebrating our victory in style with a wide selection of ales, and our coach was forced to stop in Boston for us to answer the call of nature. Ten miles further on, immersed in a particularly interesting video, we realised that we'd left one of our party behind. Backtracking, we failed to find him, so we guessed that he had managed to hitch a lift in a car or on another coach.

Unknown to us, he had managed to get on another coach that was only going as far as the Larkman pub, some distance from County Hall where his car was parked. As the weather had become even worse, he decided he'd try and flag down our coach as it passed. His ingenious idea was to push the pedestrian crossing button whenever a coach approached, forcing it to stop at the lights. Apparently, after he'd done this about four or five times, a blue-uniformed figure emerged from the shadows and asked him in no uncertain terms what he was playing at. As he searched for a plausible explanation, he saw our coach go sailing past, with no-one on board even realising that he was standing by the road, a long walk back to County Hall ahead of him!

51

The perfect day

Norwich City 2–0 Ipswich Town ⚽ Milk Cup semi-final, second leg ⚽ 6 March 1985

By Keith Webb

Keith's association with City began in October 1978 when he became a non-contract player with the Youth Team. In his second season he was a member of John Benson's South East Counties League-winning team, playing alongside John Fashanu, Mark Barham and Paul Haylock. Keith is currently in charge of the reserve team at Carrow Road.

Steve Bruce celebrates after heading the Canaries to Wembley

1985

The Milk Cup semi-final second leg against Ipswich at Carrow Road was a tremendous night for everyone connected to Norwich City. We were trailing one-nil from the first leg, when we could easily have lost by three or four. The scene was perfectly set.

After finishing my duties in the box office, I watched the game from within the burnt-out main stand. John Deehan put us on level terms in the first half, which in terms of commitment and aggression is unsurpassed in my memory.

The game was heading towards extra-time when Steve Bruce scored the winning goal at the Barclay End. Those last two or three minutes after that goal were unforgettable. The fans were making so much noise you could hardly hear yourself think. At the final whistle it was chaos as the realisation of reaching Wembley sank in. It was not until several hours later that I realised what that would mean for me personally, selling all those tickets for the final, but it was well worth it!

52

Every silver lining has a cloud

Norwich City 1–0 Sunderland ✪ Milk Cup Final ✪ 24 March 1985

By Rob Emery

Rob describes here the Milk Cup Final of 1985, and the emotion of watching his team at Wembley. Rob first saw the Canaries in action at Carrow Road on 28 November 1978 when they lost to Everton.

To many Norwich fans, beating Ipswich over two legs in the semi-final of the 1984/5 League Cup was a greater reward than a trip to Wembley for the final itself. Not so for this fan. Having never been to Wembley before, let alone to watch my own side play, my initial thoughts when Steve Bruce's bullet header brought George Burley to his knees with just three minutes left in the second leg turned more to Wembley than to mocking that lot from down the road.

I was fifteen at the time, and I ask forgiveness for this unfortunate aberration in an otherwise blameless Norwich supporting career. In 1985, however, the myth that was Wembley seemed a wonderful thing. Those were the days of 100,000 capacity, crowds swaying on the end terraces, no Olympic gallery to block the view – and those wooden bench seats in the lower seating tiers that were almost guaranteed to give you splinters. The princely sum of £12 got you a chance to take a small, if painful, piece of Wembley away with you.

It was actually fortunate that I'd made it at all. Standing on a windy forecourt five miles from home, waiting to board the coach provided free of charge by my father's usual builders' merchants, my father suddenly realised that he'd left the

The triumphant City players start their lap of honour at Wembley

match tickets lying on the kitchen table. We remained in place for the best part of half an hour, ready to throw ourselves in front of the wheels if the coach driver even dared consider leaving, while he returned home to rectify a panic-inducing situation.

Kick-off time was approaching by the time we drew into the car park. To my great chagrin, therefore, I missed the walk up Wembley Way, the 150-a-side match between Norwich and Sunderland supporters in the car park, and much of the camaraderie that seemed unique to those from Norfolk and Wearside. My enforced choice was to scamper for one of the few toilets on the concourse before climbing the steps and entering the stadium. I settled in my seat, almost level with the goal-line, forty-five minutes before kick-off.

1985

Watching your own club in a Cup Final of any description, particularly for the first time, should really be such a memorable occasion that every detail is committed to memory for instant recall years later. Sadly, the intervening years have dulled the old grey cells somewhat. I can recall Everton's winning goal in my first ever game at Carrow Road with great clarity, yet have been able to retain only sketchy details from this far more uplifting experience years later.

The obvious things, clearly, do stick – there's John Deehan robbing David Corner on the goal-line, transferring the ball to Asa Hartford, and his effort deflecting off Gordon Chisholm to go in. Next up, Dennis Van Wyk (competing with Barry Venison for most ridiculous haircut of the day) needlessly handling just minutes later, but Clive Walker stroking his penalty against the outside of the post – with me convinced Chris Woods would save it anyway. Finally, Dave Watson turning towards us from the balcony with the cup, followed by the photograph and the lap of honour.

Then there's the minutiae that really shouldn't matter but somehow become so important – like me announcing how many minutes were left, every minute, for the last twenty minutes. That must have been annoying for anyone sitting around me.

Coming out afterwards, practically all the Sunderland fans were magnificent in defeat, many taking time to congratulate us on the way out – although frankly that hardly came as a surprise. As rival coaches passed each other on the crawl from the car park, we exchanged waves – until a Sunderland coach containing some rather inebriated fans broke any illusions I might have had that football was always like this by aiming some rather less convivial gestures in our direction!

The thought of European football for the first time hadn't yet sunk in, but it was taken away anyway within weeks; Liverpool fans rioted at Heysel and the ban on English clubs was enforced. Not only that, relegation followed, as Coventry were scandalously allowed to play three fixtures after everyone else had finished.

Every silver lining has a cloud – but as Wembley '85 remains City's only Cup Final appearance in my supporting lifetime, I wouldn't have swapped it for anything.

53

Singing in the rain

Chelsea 1–2 Norwich City ◉ First Division ◉ 14 May 1985

By Kevan Platt

Kevan is the Canaries' current Club Secretary who saw his first Norwich match in October 1968 as the Canaries took on Crystal Palace. The co-author of the Centenary Edition of *Canary Citizens*, Kevan recalls a memorable night at Stamford Bridge in 1985.

Club secretary Kevan Platt (right) pictured here with one of his predecessors, Bert Westwood, recalls the rain-soaked win at Stamford Bridge as his most memorable match

We had won the Milk Cup and clinched a place in Europe, but our league form had slumped and relegation was looming. The game against Chelsea should never have been played; there were puddles all over the pitch and passing the ball was virtually impossible. It was probably too late in the season to re-arrange the game.

I stood at the open end with all the other City fans and I have never been so wet. We were all soaked to the skin; the torrential rain never stopped.

Asa Hartford put us in the lead, scoring after John Deehan's penalty had been saved. Chelsea equalised and the score stayed at one-one until the last couple of minutes. If we had drawn, Coventry would have needed to win two of their last three games to condemn us to relegation. If we won, Coventry would need to win all three of their games, a seemingly impossible task.

The rest is history, as they say. Steve Bruce scored to give us a vital victory. The fans were delirious – wet but happy. It was a great journey home and we all thought we were safe. However, wins over Luton and Stoke gave Coventry a chance of survival.

May 1985 must have been the bleakest month ever for Norwich fans.

Coventry punished the recently crowned champions Everton for their apparent lack of effort one Sunday morning, and just a few days later Liverpool fans rioted at the Heysel Stadium and our European dream was snatched away – a sickening way to be denied our rightful place in the UEFA Cup.

For my next memorable match a winning FA Cup Final appearance would be nice, or even an away win at Portman Road to clinch the championship. Dreams maybe, but who knows?

Debut delight

Norwich 2–1 Tottenham Hotspur ☾ First Division ☾ 8 November 1986

By Bryan Gunn

One-time babysitter for Alex Ferguson's children, Norwich goalkeeper for more than 12 years, Scottish International and Sheriff of Norwich, Bryan, the Club's Sponsorship Sales Manager, is undoubtedly one of the most talented and best-loved players ever to don the Canaries strip.

My arrival at Norwich in October 1986 was actually slightly later than both Norwich and I had hoped. The deal was arranged in August but an early season injury to Aberdeen's first choice keeper Jim Leighton delayed it. I played six or seven games for Aberdeen before Jim returned to fitness, but at least it gave Norwich a chance to see me in senior action. An injury to Graham Berstead enabled me to make my senior debut for Norwich in a Full Members Cup tie against Coventry. City won that match two-one in front of 6,235 fans. But the next game, just four days later at home to Tottenham, is my most memorable.

Having only played about twenty first-team matches in my career at the time, my league debut for Norwich in the game against Spurs, with around 22,000 inside the ground, was a big occasion for me. I think we were lying fifth in the table at the time, challenging teams like Forest, Arsenal and Liverpool. Ray Clemence was in goal for Spurs, and it was a thrill to be playing against one of my boyhood heroes. It was a fast match with Ian Crook scoring the deciding goal in our two-one win.

Our next two games were a goalless home draw with Manchester United and a four-one home defeat by Everton in the League Cup.

Playing in so many big games early in my Norwich career helped me to settle quickly. It was a tremendous experience for me to be playing regularly opposite the likes of Clemence, Shilton and Southall.

Having arrived from Aberdeen Bryan recalls his league debut against Spurs as one of his favourite matches

The best football at Carrow Road

Norwich City 8–0 Sutton United ⚽ FA Cup, fourth round ⚽ 28 January 1989

By Jason Masala

Jason made his debut as a supporter on 8 November 1980 when Norwich beat Everton at home.

After their famous victory over Coventry City in the FA Cup, the non-leaguers of Sutton United made headline news across the country. Charismatic manager Barrie Williams was lapped up by the press, while goal-scoring heroes Tony Rains and Matthew Hanlan even appeared on Wogan. But now everybody wanted to know who they would face next.

As I got ready for school on a dank Monday morning, the genial Williams sat on the Breakfast TV sofa to watch the fourth round draw. As Norwich City's name came out of the hat, I just knew which team would follow them. Williams' face was a picture. With a wry smile and a shake of the head, the man who quoted Kipling in his team talks knew the party would soon be over.

The talk that day from my glory-hunting friends was that Norwich would be the next victim of Williams' master plan. However, I knew better. That season Dave Stringer's men were playing the best football ever seen at Carrow Road, and were gunning for a league and cup double. When Sutton came to visit, City lay second in the (old) Division One.

Thousands travelled from the Surrey town. Many Chelsea and Ipswich fans apparently made up the numbers, which explains why I spent the early stages ducking coins in the Barclay End. The gate was a near-full house of 23,000. Only the likes of Arsenal, Liverpool and Manchester United attracted more at Carrow Road that season. Media interest was huge. It was seen as the tie of the round in many quarters and was Match of the Day's main game that night.

Any hopes the headline-writers had of another cup sensation were dashed instantly. Piling the pressure on right from the start, City were two-nil up within fifteen minutes. Scorers Trevor Putney and Malcolm Allen had effectively finished the game as a contest.

Robert Fleck's party piece just before the break added to the celebratory mood on the terraces. An outrageous chip from thirty yards (it seemed even further out from where I was standing) left keeper Trevor Roffey stranded. The goal was so good it even made the opening credits of Grandstand for the rest of the season.

At half-time, people on the Barclay were taking bets with each other on how

Malcolm hit four as the Canaries avoided an upset against Sutton United

many Norwich would score. I'd already clinched my winnings from a foolish school friend who wagered on a Sutton victory. The club record of ten-two from the 1930s was potentially in sight, especially when Allen and Fleck made it five within minutes of the restart.

In the end they settled for eight. Allen and Fleck ended up with four and three goals apiece. It should have been many many more but City gamely spared Sutton any further embarrassment. Match of the Day's edited highlights never showed the full extent of Norwich's domination. Yet Sutton were not humiliated, and played their hearts out. Against a weaker outfit they may have come much closer, but Norwich were simply brilliant, playing on a different plane from them.

Sutton left the field to an emotional ovation the like of which I've never seen before or since at Carrow Road. The whole ground was on its feet as the non-leaguers took their deserved lap of honour. It would be easy to belittle City's victory as simply thrashing a poor side (as my fickle friends did) but how many 8–0 wins have there been in the FA Cup since?

For me this game remains memorable because it epitomised the high points of the Dave Stringer era. The football was attacking, the defence uncompromising. There was some outstanding individual talent: Gunn, Townsend, Gordon and Fleck were the pick of the bunch, but there were few duff players under Stringer's management that season.

The party atmosphere made the day a memorable one for both sets of fans. Yet as 'On the ball, City' filled the air, few would have foreseen the spectre of Hillsborough only weeks later in the same competition. The jam-packed terraces at Carrow Road that day would soon be a thing of the past.

Norwich never got their double. Fourth place and an FA Cup semi-final was scant reward for City's efforts, while the European ban denied Stringer the glory that would eventually come Mike Walker's way. Meanwhile Sutton United and the charming Williams disappeared back into obscurity. They would never be forgotten though, at least not by the thousands who crammed into Carrow Road that cold January day.

56

City turn on the style

Norwich City 8–0 Sutton United ⚽ FA Cup fourth round ⚽ 28 January 1989

By Mark Cracknell

Canary fan Mark Cracknell, a real lover of Cup-ties had no hesitation in naming the 8-0 FA Cup triumph over Sutton United in 1989 as his favourite moment from City's Century.

I shouldn't have to justify selecting an eight-nil victory as a favourite match, but it was against a non-league team and one we really ought to have won anyway. It wasn't so much the margin of victory that meant so much – although it was a thrilling attacking performance – more that it was one of the highpoints of a campaign that promised so much and, in the end, delivered so little.

To put it into context, we were in the middle of a fine season. I think we were second in the league – the old First Division – to Arsenal, having led for most of the first half of the campaign. The defence of Bryan Gunn, Ian Culverhouse, Mark Bowen, Andy Linighan and Ian Butterworth had been excellent, more than compensating for a slight lack of goals from Robert Fleck, Robert Rosario and Malcolm Allen. If anything, the away form had been better than the performances at Carrow Road.

We had beaten Port Vale three-one away in the FA Cup third round, thanks largely to two superb Andy Townsend goals; Sutton, rather more memorably, had beaten Coventry two-one. Between the two rounds, the Sky Blues had beaten us two-one at Carrow Road, so – in theory – the match might not have been that straightforward.

At least, that's what the booking office clerk at Stowmarket hoped. 'It's an awfully long way to go and see them lose,' he said in his broad Suffolk accent (and yes, I am a Suffolk Canary). His hopes for the result would doubtless have been echoed by all the Ipswich fans who came up on the same train as me. Our then lower-division friends from Portman Road were without a game that day, having been knocked out in the third round.

For the first few minutes, it looked as though they might have had a case, as Sutton looked quite useful. Then we scored twice in a couple of minutes around the quarter-hour; Trevor Putney's volley after a corner was deflected in, and Allen climaxed a sweeping move, just beating the despairing dive of a Surrey defender after Dale Gordon's shot had been blocked by visiting keeper Trevor Roffey.

The third, killer goal arrived a few minutes before half-time, Robert Fleck accepting Bowen's pass and, without breaking stride, chipping Roffey from outside the box.

I don't know what Dave Stringer said at half-time, but after the break we really turned on the style and hammered home our advantage (and how often have we ever been able to say that?) with the added bonus that we were playing towards the River End, where I was standing.

Within a minute of the restart Malcom Allen headed home a near-post cross. Fleck then completed his hat-trick. His second was a shot which Roffey fumbled in but after his third, when he rounded the keeper and rolled the ball home, the Sutton number one actually shook the Scottish striker's hand.

Flecky celebrates his hat-trick in the 8–0 win over Sutton United

Like Fleck's second, Allen's third was one of the less memorable goals of the afternoon; he seemed to slightly mis-hit a volley beyond Roffey. But his fourth goal, and our last, saw a wonderful cameo from substitute Ian Crook. His drag-back fooled an opponent and gave him the time and space to flight a ball into Allen's path. It was so perfect that Allen still had time to lob it over the advancing Roffey after missing it at his first attempt.

And that was the end of that. I think the PA announcer said it was our record FA Cup victory. Either way, the Sutton players did a lap of honour after the match and were applauded off the pitch. Barrie Williams, the Shakespeare-quoting manager, still wore a broad smile at the final whistle. Robert Chase, in his chairman's programme notes on the day and afterwards, managed to out-quote Williams ('Enough. No more. 'Tis not so sweet now as it was before', with apologies to the Bard and *The Tempest*) and rightly claimed we were a credit to the First Division.

However, the story does not have a happy ending. We went on to beat Sheffield United and West Ham in the following rounds before going down one-nil to Everton at Villa Park in the semi-finals on a day when everyone remembers the other tie at Hillsborough. By that stage our league form had collapsed and we (only!) finished fourth.

Still. I do hope the Ipswich fans enjoyed the game – and the booking clerk enjoyed the result.

57

In the shadow of Hillsborough

Norwich City 0–1 Everton ☙ FA Cup semi-final ☙ 15 April 1989

By Mark Burchett

A Canaries fan for over 30 years, Mark here describes a match when the the final score was transcended by the greatest tragedy in English football history. Anyone who remembers the events of 15 April 1989 will, like Mark, recall how rivalries and results were forgotten as respect was paid to fellow supporters, irrespective of their allegiance.

My memories of this game are for all the wrong reasons, and not just because of the defeat either!

For while Everton denied Norwich their first ever appearance at an FA Cup final at the home of Aston Villa, the tie between Liverpool and Nottingham Forest at Sheffield Wednesday's ground will forever be known for the Hillsborough tragedy.

Ninety-six people tragically lost their lives from overcrowding in Sheffield that day. It was a watershed for our great game, and was to herald the all-seater stadium, designed to ensure that such a disaster never happens again.

Meanwhile, in Birmingham, it was City's first FA Cup semi-final for exactly thirty years, enabling me to experience what the fans of 1959 must have enjoyed when their Division Three heroes reached the same stage. City weren't nearly as much the underdogs this time round. In fact, the Toffees finished below the Canaries in the league! And on the back of City's best ever finish in the league (fourth in the old Division One), fans' expectations going into the game were understandably high.

Me and my wife at the time, Jacqueline, were among over 10,000 fanatical standing fans packed into the old Holte End at Villa Park. I shall never forget the sight of so many bright yellow inflatable Canaries, many of which had been proudly displayed in the cars, vans, minibuses and coaches carrying the 20,000-plus Norwich fans that created a line of yellow along the M6. Nor shall I forget the many rousing choruses of 'On the ball, City' that echoed inside the old stand, making the hairs on the back of my neck stand on end.

Unfortunately, City were unable to secure their passage to the final. Canary fans were denied the sight of their talismanic Scottish striker Robert Fleck, who – rightly – travelled home on the eve of the game to be with his family, as his father had passed away.

On the pitch the sides cancelled each other out, neither taking control of the game. Much of the action was played out in midfield and there was little goalmouth action, with the Norfolk side unfortunately the worst culprits.

I think that, like the fans, the players were overawed by the occasion and never really reached the heights we had all hoped for. In the end a Pat Nevin

The inflatable Canaries greet the team on to the pitch at Villa Park

goal sealed the Canaries' fate. It was rough justice for City boss Dave Stringer, who had produced a team renowned throughout the country for its style and quality of passing football.

During the game news had filtered through that the game at Hillsborough had been abandoned, initially it was said because of crowd disturbances, but as we reached our cars and listened eagerly to the radios we were to learn the horrible truth.

Ironically, we had planned to spend the rest of the weekend with my wife's parents in Widnes, Cheshire, part of the footballing hotbed that supports either Liverpool or Everton, loyalties even dividing some households. So we headed off up the M6. I shall never forget the strange feeling of driving amongst fans who by rights should have been celebrating their side's victory but were left wondering whether they too lost a friend or loved one.

In some ways I felt honoured to be able to share in the grief that engulfed the whole community. The home of Liverpool, Anfield, became a shrine of thousands of flowers where football fans, whether they had lost anyone they knew or not, paid their respects. It is with no joy that I say nobody I knew died.

I think when the FA Cup final did eventually take place at Wembley, it was fitting that it was between the two Merseyside giants, as the whole of the country watched in sympathy. Liverpool might have won the game three-two, after extra time, but in reality there were no winners, just losers, as ninety-six innocent people had lost their lives. The fact that Norwich had been beaten in the semi-final was almost irrelevant.

58

English football's saddest day

Norwich City 0–1 Everton ◐ FA Cup semi-final ◐ 15 April 1989

By Ben Hawksley

Ben has been a die-hard City fan since then mid-70s and retains his love of the Club despite now living in South London.

It was a bright sunny day and I was looking forward to our first FA Cup semi since 1959. We had avoided Liverpool in the draw, so my hopes were up – I had a good feeling that we could get to Wembley.

I went to the ground with my dad and we got there early. We were standing at the Holte End, and by 2pm our side of the Holte End was packed with excited Canary fans – and twice as many inflatable canaries! It struck me as odd that the parts of the ground designated for the Everton fans remained largely empty until much nearer kick-off, when they were soon filled and we were all ready.

We were quite near the pitch, so we were only really able to see the action at our end. The players seemed nervous from the start. Things got worse when, right in front of us, Ian Crook tried to clear a harmless-looking cross but only managed to put it on to our cross-bar. In what seemed like slow motion the ball dropped to Pat Nevin and he scored for Everton – nightmare! The rest of the first half saw us create no real chances. Our players seemed really tense and by half-time we had only managed one long-range effort, from Dale Gordon.

At half-time the electronic scoreboard displayed news from the other semi-final between Liverpool and Nottingham Forest at Hillsborough – start delayed. Rumours went round that there had been some crowd trouble, which had delayed kick-off.

The second half started, and we continued to struggle to create anything. We had Robert Rosario up front, and I remember his best chance coming from a cross from our right. He climbed at the far post to head, but at the crucial moment he closed his eyes as the sun fell on them at just the wrong moment. As the second half continued more rumours circulated about the other semi – five people had been killed, but it was unconfirmed. The tension on the pitch still held our concentration.

When the final whistle went we were all gutted. If we were honest, we knew we had not played well, but neither had Everton, and nil-nil would not have been unfair on either side. The excitement of the Milk Cup in

A ticket stub from the Norwich section of the Holte End

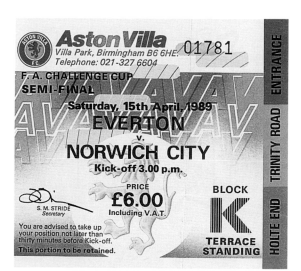

1985 was still fresh and I think many City fans saw this as another Wembley day out. We trudged back to the car for the drive home, debating what had cost us the game.

The other semi was still in the back of our minds and as we got in the car we put on Radio Two for Sports Report. It was then that our moods changed. It was just before 5pm, and the report said that seventy-five people had been killed in the Liverpool end at Hillsborough, crushed to death as supporters tried to get into the ground. It was several minutes before either of us spoke. Having spent the last three hours stood on a terrace very similar to the one at the Leppings Lane end of Hillsborough, it was a real shock. Our result and performance were truly put in perspective. It was the saddest day football in England has ever known – the final death toll reached ninety-six. After that day, following your favourite team changed for ever, so, as we celebrate a hundred good and bad years, it will stick in my mind alongside Bayern Munich, the Ipswich Milk Cup semi-final and many other great Norwich performances.

59

Taming the Red Devils

Manchester United 0–2 Norwich City ☾ First Division ☾ 30 August 1989

By David Machin

Lancashire-lad David took the local team to his heart when he moved to Norwich in 1988, investing in a season ticket immediately on his arrival and remaining loyal to his adopted Club throughout the highlights and disappointments of the last 14 years.

When I was asked to write about my favourite Norwich City game, I didn't think it would be that difficult. I have been supporting City since 1988, when I moved here from Blackpool, and unfortunately, as we all know, the last seven years have not been that memorable. But when I sat down to choose I realised that in fact it wouldn't be quite that easy. I could have chosen a match from the European days, including the defeat of mighty Bayern Munich (let's hope those days return), the 1992 FA Cup run, or our record-breaking season of 1992/93. But if one game stands out more than any other, it is Manchester United–Norwich City at Old Trafford on 30 August 1989.

I didn't start supporting Norwich City until I was twenty-four, and the reason was that I was born and bred in Blackpool. While a lot of the locals would jump in their cars for a thirty-five-mile journey to see Liverpool or Manchester, I was a regular at Bloomfield Road watching the Tangerines, and boy did I get a lot of stick for it.

To cut a very long story short, I met my then-wife-to-be on holiday in Greece and a five-year romance followed (you can't rush these things) before we were engaged and finally moved to Norwich, my wife's home, in the summer of 1988. I am a firm believer in supporting your local team, so one of my first jobs was to invest in a season ticket for the one and only Norwich City Football Club.

I was excited at the prospect of watching top-flight football for the first time in my life, but I wasn't expecting that much from Norwich. They had only just avoided relegation the previous season, and I thought they would have a hard struggle to avoid the drop this time. How wrong could I be? A fantastic season followed, in which we played some of the most entertaining football I have ever seen and almost finished with the league title. My team was one of the top footballing teams in the country – my team was Norwich City!

One of the highlights of the close season is the release of the forthcoming season's fixtures. Like most fans, I study the fixtures to see when we will be playing the so-called big teams, and pick the away matches I will attend. When Norwich are playing in the north-west I try to visit my parents on the same trip, so when I saw that the fourth match was against Manchester United, I thought this would be a great time to go to Old Trafford for the first time. My dad said he would love to come and watch the game with me, and to my astonishment even my wife wanted to go. So three tickets were purchased for my wife's first football match, and my and my dad's first visit to the home of Manchester United.

The programme from City's 2–0 win at Old Trafford in 1989

Norwich started the season with a two-nil win at Sheffield Wednesday, followed by two home draws, to Nottingham Forest and QPR. Manchester United started their season with a four-one win over champions Arsenal. They had made many new signings, including Mike Phelan, Norwich's captain from last season, and the day before the game they had paid Middlesborough £2.3 million for Gary Pallister – a record fee for a defender at the time. We talked to some Man United fans before the game; they were so confident, it was untrue. They thought it was just a case of turning up to collect the points, and that another four-one victory was on the cards. I politely pointed out to them that we had done the double over them last season, and they would find out in the next two hours how easy it would be. As we made our way to the ground through all the hot-dog vendors' vans, the smell of onions mixed with anticipation and excitement. Would it be our night? Would we get the points? Would we beat Manchester United?

Once in the ground the atmosphere was starting to build, and when the teams came out the noise was electric. The 700 or so who had made the journey from Norfolk were in fine voice, but it was going to be hard to compete with the masses from Manchester. As expected, United started very well, and after only five minutes Bryan Gunn was called into action to save a shot from Neil Webb. A crescendo of noise echoed around Old Trafford. 'They may be right,' said my dad. 'It might be four-one after all.'

Norwich settled down and started to pass the ball well. Then, just before half-time, an up-field ball by Andy Townsend was headed down by Robert Fleck and split the defence. Dale Gordon ran through and Jim Leighton came out to meet him, but 'Disco' Gordon was too quick and slotted the ball into the net to make it one-nil. The Stretford End went very quiet, while us away fans went mad with excitement. Even my dad was cheering, and my wife – well!

Half-time arrived and we cheered the lads off the pitch. Was it a dream? We had outplayed Manchester United for forty-five minutes, and taken the lead. I wanted the game to be over right then. Manchester would surely come at us hard in the next forty-five minutes – would we be able to hold on to our lead?

To be honest, most of the second half is a blur. You know what it's like: I kept looking at my watch, wishing the time away, hoping we could hold on. Then, with about fifteen minutes to go, Ian Crook sent a ball through to Robert Rosario who got into the penalty area, went past Gary Pallister (making his debut) and was brought down. I looked at the referee – and he pointed to the spot. A penalty to Norwich, a penalty to the away team at Old Trafford! Blimey, what's going on? I had to pinch myself. The home fans were booing the decision – what was the ref thinking?

The Norwich fans stood and looked at Robert Fleck. Could he do it? I clenched my fists together and I remember thinking 'come on Flecky, let's silence these Reds'. Flecky ran up and – Yessss! – the ball hit the corner of the goal. At two-nil it was party time on the terraces. The feeling can't be described, but all you football fans out there know what I mean. It's like birthday, Christmas, and new year all rolled into one. As the home fans headed for the exits Flecky nearly made it three, but his header was cleared off the line. Finally the referee blew for full time. Away fans delirious, home fans despondent – we had won at Old Trafford.

While many Norwich fans had that long journey home I had the relatively short trip to Blackpool, with my dad praising us up. 'You just might win something this season,' he said. Unfortunately we didn't but at least I had a team to be proud of. Hopefully we will be back in the Premiership soon, but I was there when we last won at Old Trafford, I was there.

60

A game that had it all

Arsenal 4–3 Norwich City ○ First Division ○ 4 November 1989

By James Blower

A fan since the age of six, and a Club mascot at 13, James has witnessed many memorable moments of NCFC history since his first attendance in a 1983 Division One game against Manchester United.

The programme from the infamous 'Highbury Brawl' in November 1989

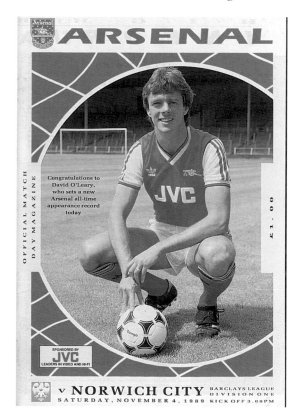

I had just celebrated my thirteenth birthday and the club had allowed me the honour of being mascot for the game at Highbury. I travelled to the game with my dad, NCISA's Roy Blower, and my friend William Beck, another keen Norwich fan. Having been mascot at Carrow Road the previous season when Norwich had played Arsenal's north London rivals Tottenham, I knew what the experience of going onto the pitch would be like. I remembered the advice of my PE teacher, Mr Wright, who had told me after the Tottenham game that my job was to warm up the goalkeeper, not to put as many as I could past Bryan Gunn! Therefore, I put in as many useful shots as I could – my reward was to get as much of the ball as Malcolm Allen (who was also helping get 'Gunny' into shape).

The game was delayed for a presentation to David O'Leary, who was making a record 622nd appearance for Arsenal at thirty-one. He was given a shirt with '622' on it to mark the occasion, and shots of me with David, Ian Butterworth, the Arsenal mascot and the officials were shown around the world that night on television.

Norwich were sitting in sixth place in the league, behind the Gunners who were fourth. The Canaries were keen to avenge a five-nil drubbing on live television the season before, but our chances looked slim: Arsenal were unbeaten at home and had only conceded a single goal – from Paul Goddard of Derby – at home all season.

Dave Stringer got the start he was looking for when a Dale Gordon corner was flicked on by Michael Thomas for Malcolm Allen to nod in at the back post. Allen had only started due to an injury to crowd favourite Robert Fleck.

Warming Gunny up looked to have been a waste of time when, minutes later, Smith tapped in an equaliser in the six-yard box, but the linesman rightly signalled offside. The generosity of the officials was to be short-lived: Allen soon had a goal disallowed in similar circumstances.

After twenty minutes, the lead was extended. O'Leary

brought down the dangerous Allen on the edge of the box and Dave Phillips curled a 'special' past the outstretched Lukic from twenty yards. It stayed two-nil until the fifty-fifth minute, when Gunny could only parry Kevin Richardson's free kick into the path of Niall Quinn, who slotted home his first of the season. Six minutes later and Linighan was harshly adjudged to have handled by George Tyson. Lee Dixon, taking his first ever penalty, made no mistake to level matters at two-two.

Norwich came roaring back with another Gordon corner that was met by a powerful Linighan header from sixteen yards. Lukic parried and Tim Sherwood, who had replaced Andy Townsend after the midfielder failed a fitness test, blasted home from an acute angle. Fourteen minutes left, and Norwich were looking good value for a win in an exciting game where both sides had played excellent football.

One minute later and it all went horribly wrong. O'Leary met Winterburn's free kick and Norwich had done the charitable thing that all neutrals wanted to see – capped O'Leary's day with a goal. O'Leary had only managed nine in the previous 622 games!

In stoppage time, Phillips somehow got on the end of a Culverhouse cross but with Lukic nowhere, the ball trickled past the post. Moments later, a long ball from Lukic was flicked on by Smith to Thomas. With his back to goal on the penalty spot, Thomas backed so far into Butterworth that the Norwich defender fell over. Thomas tripped over his feet and Tyson awarded the second penalty of the game.

Gunn dived to his right and pulled off a fantastic save. The cheers of the Norwich fans were cut short as the ball rolled out to Dixon, whose second effort trickled into the net. This sparked 'handbags at ten paces' between the Norwich defence and a couple of Arsenal players. Things got worse when number of Arsenal players who were congratulating Dixon on the halfway line ran half the length of the pitch to get involved, and a twenty-one-man brawl ensued.

Norwich were fined £50,000 and Arsenal £20,000 in one of the FA's great injustices. The only people impressed were Norwich sponsors Asics, who are rumoured to have called Robert Chase to 'congratulate' him on the wonderful world-wide publicity their kits had received as a result of the brawl!

A thoroughly entertaining contest had been marred by a few minutes of madness at the end. However, the game had it all – excitement, goals, great saves (mostly from Gunny), penalties, bookings, landmark appearances and fighting! It is a game I will never forget.

61

Flecky to the rescue

Exeter City 1–1 Norwich City ⚽ FA Cup third round ⚽ 6 January 1990

By Tim Skinner

Tim, like many other supporters, remains fervent in his support of the Canaries despite living a few hundred miles from Carrow Road. It's maybe the 'bouncing mass of yellow and green' or the memories of Robert Fleck's inspired brilliance. Whatever – Tim knows for sure why he loves Norwich City.

Robert Fleck's equaliser saved City at St James' Park

I knew that we were going to win the FA cup in 1990. I was determined to see every match on the way to the final. The first step to Wembley was a round trip of 600 miles to see us play fourth division Exeter City in the third round.

The journey to Exeter was planned to perfection but suffered in its execution. A 6am start in a hire car that broke down ninety minutes later in Essex. A tow truck that turned up three long hours later. The helpful and sympathetic mechanic who didn't know exactly what the problem was but did know that the car was 'completely knackered lads'. And the garage dog who menaced us because he apparently didn't like 'people in hats'.

A flurry of pre-mobile phone calls finally got us a replacement car at 1.00pm which gave us precisely two hours to travel the remaining 200 miles round the M25 and down the M5 to make kick-off at 3.00pm. Despite the proposed alternative of diverting to see Cambridge United play we decided to continue on our way to the West Country. Thanks to some very scary driving and a reckless disregard for national speed limits we were in the ground at 2.59pm. (Thanks Chris!)

After all this we felt we were entitled to a classic match, but the pitch was a mud bath and very little real football was played. As both teams became caked in mud it became increasingly difficult to tell them apart.

Deep into the second half the unthinkable happened and Exeter took the lead. The rain began to drizzle down on the open terrace where the City fans were. I could already hear the laughing and jeering in Suffolk.

Then Robert Fleck scored and I knew why I loved Norwich. In celebration he flung himself into the bouncing mass of yellow and green behind the goal for a group hug of gigantic proportions. Five minutes later, when it seemed he would never reappear, he was reluctantly prised away from the terrace by Robert Rosario to finish the game. The FA cup dream was still alive!

The match finished one all and we arrived back in Norwich just in time to miss the highlights on Match of the Day. The rest of course is history. We beat Exeter in the replay before going out to Liverpool in the next round.

62

Togetherness

FA Cup run ☾ January to April 1992

By Andrew Cullen

Andy Cullen is the Canaries'
Director of Sales and Marketing
and actually had the idea of this
publication. A life-long Canaries
fan, Andy looks back fondly on
the 1991/92 FA Cup run.

Being both a lifetime fan and enjoying the privilege of working for the club provides a plethora of topics for a collection like this. Every day brings something special. As a fan, was it that first match at Carrow Road, winning promotion, Wembley, Europe, one of those 'goalfest' thrillers? Or as an employee, that first day working at Carrow Road, or that memorable fifty-niners reunion day? Or walking up the steps at the Millennium Stadium, gazing proudly at the sea of green and yellow on the concourse, the fans singing from windows and rooftops?

In the end my contribution recalls one of the special properties that makes football so special: its ability to evoke the spirit of camaraderie, friendship, pleasure and laughter. In a word – togetherness. The FA Cup run of 1992 brought out all of those qualities. It brought together a group of friends, three of them temporary converts to the cause, who made a round trip of over 2500 miles with smiles aplenty and great fun along every mile.

At the time I was an exiled Norwich fan working in Birmingham and playing Sunday football in Kidderminster. The Hoobrook Crown FC graced the dizzy heights of Division Six of the Kidderminster and District League. I had been condemned to goalkeeping out of necessity: nobody else would play there. In the back four was another exiled Norwich fan, Hughie. We travelled together to several Norwich matches and his friendship was critical in a team split between support for the Baggies and pre-Muscat Wolves.

As members, both Hughie and I ordered our tickets for City's third-round FA Cup home tussle with Barnsley. After a Friday night Hoobrook Crown 'training session', where the skill factor was determined by ability to attract the barmaid's attention, three of our team-mates decided to join us. Giler, a versatile attacker, Kevin who as our perennial leading goalscorer proudly boasted the Golden Slipper on his mantelpiece, and Bradders, our own dodgy linesman who had been banned sine die for a moment of Sunday morning madness in 1987.

On the way the three of them pledged that if Norwich beat the Tykes they would continue to support the team, sticking with me and Hughie all the way until they were knocked out. Indeed, the members of the temporary Black Country alliance were confident that they would be returning to watching their own teams in the fourth round. But instead it was a journey that would keep us together for three months on the road that ended at Hillsborough.

The third-round tie against Barnsley saw us book a fourth-round date with Millwall through a Robert Fleck goal. But on 25 January, as we travelled along the road near Huntingdon formerly known as the A604, Danny Baker on Radio Five announced that the game was cancelled due to a frozen pitch. A hasty glance at the fixture list for alternative fayre saw us continue on to the M11 towards Upton Park to see their tie with Wrexham. We plonked ourselves on the notorious North Bank terrace, good-natured neutrals cheering at all the right

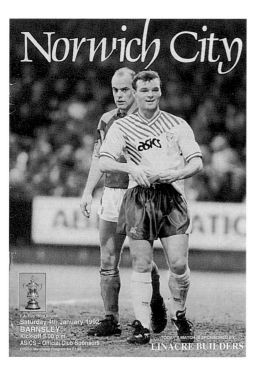

It all started at home against Barnsley

moments as Premiership Hammers gamely fought to match the skill of Third Division Welshmen – except Giler, who loudly cheered Wrexham's ninety-first-minute equaliser. The North Bank parted like the Red Sea, with Bradders and me flying off in one direction and Kev and Hughie in the other. We picked Giler up later on the Mile End Road.

Giler's disregard for his own life and career was highlighted by his decision to bunk off work ten days later so he could join us for the rearranged midweek game with Millwall. Flecky did it again, and we were on our way back for a fifth-round fixture with Notts County.

At that time Ruel Fox was struggling to hold a regular place down in the team, and Chris Sutton was just beginning his metamorphosis from assured young centre-back to goal-scoring sensation. We were in the Thorpe section, in superb front-row seats. Bradders engaged in conversation with Foxy about his prospects as he warmed up and down the touchline. The fact that Ruel had the decency to spend a good deal of time talking to Bradders, a West Brom fan, suggested a new career opening for Ruel, and it was no surprise to any of us when he eventually made it to the Hawthorns some ten years later. Meanwhile, Super Sutton scored twice to send us down the newly opened M40 towards the Dell and Southampton.

On the bright morning of March 7, close to Banbury, we tuned in to Danny Baker's Radio 5 quiz show and decided to call in on Neil's spanking new mobile, which (this being 1992) was the size of the capacious lunchbox Kevin had brought out on its annual outing. After six failed attempts to get through, we were on. Our subject was showjumping, which none of us knew anything about. Sadly we were disqualified from answering any further questions after Bradders made a rather crude response to Danny's question about the arrangement of rider and horse gold medal winners in the 1964 Olympics. It is to our intense regret that we were cruelly denied the opportunity to attend the 1992 Burleigh Horse trials as a result.

The Dell had a rather odd arrangement at the time: standing for away supporters at one end of the ground and limited seating for them at the other. For some reason we were seated midway between both. This was clearly dangerous given the previous form of both Bradders and Giler. Fortunately a nil-nil draw meant there was no nasty need for detours via Portsmouth, but it did present Giler with a another opportunity to deny his employers his services to attend another midweek replay – for a team he'd known nothing about just four months earlier.

That match was a tense affair. Despite two Southampton players, including Matt Le Tissier, being given their marching orders, Norwich huffed and puffed their way through the game with goals from Rob Newman and Chris Sutton setting Premiership Norwich up as favourites for a semi-final tie with First Division Sunderland.

The BBC's decision to show both semi-finals live on TV on Sunday presented a problem for us Sunday footballers. Our scheduled fixture was an away match at Tenbury Wells – forty miles in the wrong direction from both Kidderminster and Sheffield. The league refused our appeal to have the game rearranged – definite intransigence on their part, given the importance of both matches!

We calculated that we could get from Tenbury to Sheffield in two and a half hours with Bradders at the wheel. That meant the good burghers of Tenbury had to agree to a 9am kick-off. They did, but our own team-mates weren't too sure. Some persuasive arguments from Bradders brought everyone to heel, and we were off. Only the league were unsure, but they eventually agreed providing the match referee was happy. He wasn't, but after Bradders went to see him he was.

The next problem was match tickets. Neil and I were members, but we'd have to queue at Carrow Road, and there was no guarantee that the others would get tickets. But my work had brought me into contact with the late, great football referee Neil Midgeley, who was appointed referee for the match (I'm not sure if Bradders had anything to do with it), and he got us tickets in the directors' box.

Directors' box tickets presented another problem. Showers had not reached Tenbury Wells in 1991, and we must have looked a sight, slightly grubby in jackets and ties and as we entered the Hillsborough suite following our famous two-one win over the Tenbury tractor boys. But Bradders blagged his way in and we all followed. Sadly that was the only success of the day. Norwich simply didn't perform, and John Byrne's suspiciously offside-looking goal saw the underdogs through.

Ruel got booked after being penalised by Midge for an innocuous foul. Afterwards Bradders, in his capacity as Ruel's self-appointed advisor, asked Midge to explain himself. 'He told me that the crowd had come to watch him not me' replied Midge. 'He said I was a prima donna. I asked him for his name and he said Fox, and I then told him that I'd never heard of him but thanked him for introducing himself and letting me take a note of his name.'

Neil Midgeley was a credit to his profession, much respected by the pros. He also refereed Norwich's one-nil 1985 Milk Cup triumph, also against Sunderland, and so will always be enshrined in Norwich City history. Sadly, Neil passed away in 2000 after a short illness. The humour of the Fox incident shows a very different side to referees, which we as supporters don't often get to see.

The atmosphere on the way back was subdued and quiet. Giler, Kev and Bradders were visibly upset, showing emotions that should have been the exclusive domain of Norwich supporters like Hughie and me. I suppose we all knew that we were at the end of a very special journey of togetherness that would be difficult to repeat – after all, they had their respective loyalties to West Brom and Wolves to consider. Neil Midgeley invited me to Wembley to see the final, but it was a hollow experience.

That cup run was great because of the togetherness I had with my mates. There are many other anecdotes that I couldn't possibly commit to print, but if you ever bump into Bradders…

My favourite game

Norwich City 2–1 Southampton ⚽ FA Cup sixth round replay ⚽ 18 March 1992

By Sarah Greaves

Sarah, a science journalist, has followed NCFC since the 1988/89 season, and here recounts how an FA Cup victory over Southampton proved the perfect way to celebrate her 18th birthday.

For most people, attending a football match is probably not the first thing to do on your eighteenth birthday, especially in the evening. However, on March 18 1992 I found myself at an FA Cup sixth-round replay at Carrow Road. This has to be one of my favourite Norwich games, not only because of the result (two-one to Norwich in extra-time) but also because it was a fantastic way to celebrate turning eighteen.

A week before, on March 7, I'd attended my first ever away game, at the Dell. It maybe wasn't the ideal place to start an away-game career, and the game was a pretty dire nil-nil draw (as my Dad had cheerfully predicted it would be). I had been hoping for a Norwich victory, since I already knew that a replay would affect my birthday celebrations. But obviously there was no competition between the joys of Carrow Road and Ritzy's nightclub. My friends couldn't understand why I wanted to attend a football match when I could be having my first legal drink, but I was not to be dissuaded from watching my boys.

The day started with an announcement of my birthday in the Eastern Daily Press, telling me to enjoy my party with 22,000 others that evening. Upon reaching my seat before the game, the season-ticket holders who I sat with (and probably annoyed greatly every week, as I was the only female around for a good few rows) had bought me a card and some jammy dodgers (thanks, Ron). The evening looked promising!

Kick-off was at 7.45pm and there was a full house, with a great cup-tie atmosphere, and the game didn't disappoint. There was drama, controversy, excellent football and the classic cup-tie ingredients of a couple of red cards and a last minute goal. Although the Canaries dominated much of the first half and had many missed chances, it was the Saints who were in the lead at half-time, thanks to a Neil Ruddock goal.

Before the second half started there was an announcement over the tannoy informing all those inside the ground that it was my eighteenth birthday and – much to my embarrassment – exactly where I was sitting. All those around me turned round and wished me a happy birthday. My Dad found this all rather too amusing for my liking!

Goal! And Hillsborough beckons

I was still convinced Norwich would win – how could they let me down on my birthday? – and right from the beginning of the second half the Canaries went for the equaliser. Foxy and Gossy nearly opened the scoring, and I could sense that the tempo of the game was definitely rising. In the forty-ninth minute the game really got going when Le Tissier was sent off for kicking Robert Fleck. The tackle, we learned later, had broken two ribs.

The equaliser eventually arrived in the fifty-fourth minute. John Polston crossed the ball into the box, where a Chris Sutton header was converted by Rob Newman with an angled left-foot volley past the stranded Tim Flowers in the Southampton goal.

By the seventieth minute it was obvious that Flecky couldn't continue, and Darren Beckford was brought on as a replacement. In the minutes that followed, right up to the final whistle, the game was full of goalmouth scrambles, as the Yellows tried in vain to find the winning goal. The match was destined for extra time.

Early on in the first period of extra time another Saints player, Barry Horne, was sent off for a violent tackle on Colin Woodthorpe, but still the Canaries couldn't make the two-man advantage pay. The atmosphere by this point was tremendous, with the whole of Carrow Road up on its feet. By now, all the jammy dodgers were gone and I was beginning to feel less confident that my birthday was such a lucky charm after all.

Then, deep into the second period of extra time, just before the match would've been decided by penalties, Mark Bowen crossed, and the ball was cleared to Jeremy Goss. Gossy mis-hit his shot (something he wouldn't be doing two seasons later!) and the ball bounced to Sutton, whose looping header went over Flowers to seal the match for the Canaries. I remember celebrating wildy – what more could a girl ask for on her birthday? My favourite player of the day, Chris Sutton (and what eighteen-year-old girl in 1992 didn't think Chris Sutton was the best NCFC player?) had just scored deep into injury time, with a somewhat lucky header, to put us into the FA Cup semi-finals for the third time. It was a truly great eighteenth, not one that many other people can understand, but it is a much better story to retell than a night down the pub. Obviously the more traditional birthday celebrations were kept for the weekend following the game!

This win put us into the semi-final at Hillsborough against Sunderland, a game that is easily forgotten and only sticks in the memory for how badly we actually played and how Flecky had sat in an oxygen tank all week trying to get his ribs to heal. We all know we didn't reach the final that year – something my A-level chemistry teacher was particularly delighted about because, as he informed me the morning after the semi-final, at least I could now finally concentrate on my exams! But the season after was destined to be the greatest season ever for Norwich City fans. A great match, a great result, a great atmosphere and a great birthday.

64

The end of the Stringer era

Sunderland 1–0 Norwich City ☻ FA Cup semi-final ☻ 5 April 1992

By Mark Burchett

After describing the poignant moments of 15 April 1989, Mark here remembers the end of the Stringer era.

Having been at Norwich's FA Cup semi-final defeat against Everton on the day of the Hillsborough tragedy, it was very poignant that our next appearance in a semi-final was at the ground where that footballing disaster struck. The opponents on that day were lowly Second Division Sunderland, which unusually for City in the FA Cup made them favourites rather than underdogs!

Not only that, but the Norwich fans sat in the very same Leppings Lane stand where those ninety-six fans had so tragically and unnecessarily lost their lives. It was an eerie feeling to know I was sitting above the place where that fateful drama had taken place.

Norwich had reached their second FA Cup semi-final within three years, after disposing of Southampton in dramatic fashion in the sixth round. I can still remember the winning goal very clearly. City had already come from a goal behind when the then-teenage striker Chris Sutton scored with a looping header just minutes from the end of extra time.

After much speculation and hype, Carrow Road favourite Robert Fleck did start the Sunderland match, but was never the danger to the opposition that all City fans knew he could be. In a bid to help speed his recovery from two broken ribs, he had spent much of the days leading up to the game in a hyperbaric therapy unit.

Partnering him in attack were Chris Sutton and Ruel Fox. In goal was Mark Walton, shielded by a defensive line-up of Colin Woodthorpe, Ian Butterworth (captain), John Polston and Mark Bowen, with Ian Culverhouse playing as sweeper. Jerry Goss and Rob Newman patrolled the midfield.

Unfortunately, I can picture Sunderland's thirty-third minute winning goal all too clearly. It came from a swift right-wing counter-attack that exposed City at the back. John Byrne began the move, feeding the ball out wide in his half. He then charged through midfield towards us fans to latch perfectly on to David Rush's cross. Having wrong-footed the defence and keeper Mark Walton, Byrne had the relatively easy job of heading into pretty much an empty net.

Up to that point, City were in control of the game and giving a good account of themselves, and to go in at half-time a goal down was a body blow. After the break you couldn't fault the players' commitment as they tried to put pressure on Sunderland. Several players went close, but the ball just didn't fall kindly for them. The most notable that I remember was an effort from Sutton midway through the second half that summed up City's luck on the day. Fox and Bowen had combined well, the defender accurately finding the striker on the edge of the area. He chipped the advancing Sunderland keeper Tony Norman, and everyone in green and yellow watched in agony as the ball went just the wrong side of the bar. I'm sure all the Canary fans around me tried to suck the ball into the net! In the last minute Bowen himself had an opportunity to equalise, but the outstretched Norman saved at the bottom-right hand corner of his goal.

The Canary Choir, as they were named by an EDP journalist at the time, did their bit, singing from the Leppings Lane end until the finish. At times they even matched the massive Roker Roar from the opposite stand.

I really thought that this time, having lost out to Everton in 1989, this was our chance to reach the pinnacle of English football, a coveted FA Cup final. But yet again Norwich City couldn't do it on the big stage, shattering my dreams. And it's true, nobody ever remembers the FA Cup semi-final losers!

That defeat was the last straw for Dave Stringer, who had re-established City as a respectable quality passing side over his five-year managerial reign, but now felt he could take them no further and gallantly resigned.

The Canaries warm up prior to kick-off at Hillsborough

The game was a repeat of the 'friendly final' (City's one-nil League Cup win over Sunderland in 1985): the atmosphere between the fans at Sheffield was just as friendly, with no animosity shown by City supporters towards their north-east conquerors – just as football should be!

1992

65

Bryan Gunn – legend

Norwich City 2–1 Queen's Park Rangers ◔ Premier League ◔ 17 October 1992

By Shaun Otway

Canaries' fan Shaun Otway looks back at a time when one man put an indescribable family tragedy to one side to keep goal for the Canaries.

Gunny returns to work and a legend is born

I have many abiding memories from my years supporting Norwich since 1970, but two stand out. The number one event was not really about football. On this grey, soulless day in the famous 1992/93 season, Bryan Gunn ran out to play in goal. Yet just a few days earlier, his daughter had died. The courage of the man was beyond words. His reception will live long in the memory, and a legend was born. Norwich fans may not always show the same degree of passion that you get with other teams, but on that day, we were all pulling for Bryan. It was some season, but this is the City moment I will always remember. Oh, and the other one is easy. Milk Cup semi-final, Norwich two, Ipswich nil. Say no more!

Committed to the Canary cause

Norwich City 4–2 Leeds United ● Premier League ● 14 April 1993

By Tim Cook

Tim's first Canaries match was their final league game of the 1978/79 season. They won 1–0 at home to league runners-up Nottingham Forest.

When I was asked to write an article on a memorable match I've experienced over the years, the first game that came into my head was Norwich versus Leeds at the end of the 1992/93 season. Now, I've seen many a Norwich game and experienced some massive highs and lows, but I think this particular game came at a point in my life when football started to take priority over any other interest, setting a dangerous precedent for future campaigns.

It probably wasn't the best game of football I've ever watched, or even greatest result, but memorable games don't always mean memorable results – they're usually unique because of the circumstances that surround them. And that was the case here, because it was a game where I learnt what being a true supporter was all about.

The game was significant to me for a number of reasons, and no doubt most of you reading this will immediately recognise that this season was the club's most successful ever. It was during this particular season that, as a thirteen-year-old, I became totally immersed in the hysteria that engulfed Norfolk. I found myself wanting to go to as many games as possible, buy all the new merchandise and basically pledge my allegiance to the Canary cause. All this came to a head against Leeds that particular Wednesday evening at Carrow Road.

First and foremost, it was the first time I had been in the Barclay End. For years I had wanted to go in, particularly when it was terracing, but as my Dad paid for the tickets we sat where he wanted. He eventually gave in, probably to contain my whining, and purchased three tickets for the Barclay End, Block D.

Walking down to the ground that night I'm not sure whether I was excited or not, because I felt sick with nerves. As most of my family would testify, this is a usual symptom that accompanies any game of importance, and to me this was one of them. It was important because I felt that it was a game we had to win to keep up with Aston Villa and maintain our quest for a European place, at a time when it was still an achievement to qualify for the UEFA Cup. Furthermore, we were playing the reigning champions, and though the season had been a disaster by their standards, they still had plenty of quality in their squad.

Walking up the steps into the Barclay End I got a huge shock. Firstly, the view was completely different from the South Stand, where I had mostly been before, but more than anything I found myself submerged in a sea of noise. 'On the ball, City' was ringing in my ears as I took my seat, and I distinctly remember an enormous wave of pride running through me.

The game itself is pretty much a blur to me now, apart from vivid recollections of all the goals. We went one-nil down after a couple of minutes, as Lee Chapman finished off a sweeping Leeds move. Enter Chris Sutton, who equalised after eleven minutes before adding a second soon after, rising above the oncoming John Lukic who could do nothing to stop a powerful downward header. A minute later we were awarded a penalty. I don't know if it's just me, but whenever we get a penalty I always feel that the law of probability says we will miss. Thankfully this time I was wrong. David Phillips shot to the right of Lukic, whose valiant attempt was not quite enough to stop the ball crossing the line.

Surrounding the first-half action I gained my education in sitting in the Barclay. I learnt all the words to 'On the ball, City' as well as all other commonly sung chants. I also learnt the art of taunting individual players. In particular, I remember Lee Chapman getting all sorts of abuse about his wife having had an alleged fling with a certain Mr Cantona. Dad enjoyed that one!

Chris Sutton helped himself to a hat-trick as City floor Leeds 4–2

The second half pretty much summed up being a Norwich supporter. What should have been a comfortable half turned tense through a Rod Wallace screamer soon after half-time, before Chris Sutton rounded off a superb hat-trick with a beautifully taken goal late on in the match, slotting the ball in from a tight angle having rounded Lukic. We had won four-two.

One distinct memory from that half was when Rod Wallace scored to make the scoreline three-two. Seconds after the ball had crashed into the back of the net my friend Nick turned to me and said something along the lines of 'that was one hell of a goal'. I looked at him in disbelief. 'How can it be a great goal if it's scored against us?' I replied. He shrugged his shoulders and said no more.

Well, the drama was over and we had secured another valuable three points in a style that was customary that season – very attacking, with plenty of movement and eye-catching passes, if a little cavalier at the back. As we walked over the river and back to our car, surrounded by thousands of fellow Canaries, I thought to myself, 'surely happiness doesn't come better than this'. When I turned to my dad and said 'that was the best game I've ever watched!', I genuinely meant it. It wasn't the performance, the atmosphere or even the result. It was that I experienced everything that football is about on that Wednesday evening. The passion, the highs, the lows, the singing, the taunting, the elation as we scored and the feeling that at that moment I had 20,000 new friends.

And that is why Norwich versus Leeds in 1993 is my most memorable game.

67

It was the first match of Norwich's 80th season. Norwich lost 2–0 at home to Manchester City, but for David Thornhill it was the first of many memorable Canary moments.

Qualifying for Europe

Middlesbrough 3–3 Norwich City ☾ Premier League ☾ 8 May 1993

By David Thornhill

I have supported Norwich City from my first game, back in August 1982, and choosing a favourite was never going to be easy. There are so many good games, from the first time I saw Norwich win – Birmingham City five-one in September 1982 – to Marc Libbra's great arrival against Manchester City in August 2001. But if one game stands out it is 8 May 1993 – Norwich away to Middlesbrough on my eighteenth birthday.

The aim of the match was simple. Norwich had to avoid defeat to clinch third place in the Premiership. Then, if Arsenal could beat Sheffield Wednesday in the

FA Cup Final, Norwich would qualify for the UEFA Cup, as Arsenal had already qualified for Europe.

The week before, Norwich had beaten Liverpool one-nil, whilst Blackburn lost three-one to Manchester United. We had one game left and seventy-one points. Blackburn had two games left and sixty-five points, plus a superior goal difference. The midweek game was Blackburn away to Spurs. Unless Blackburn won, they couldn't catch us. I would be able to celebrate my eighteenth birthday with a big party at Ayresome Park, Middlesbrough. I was glued to my radio that night, but unfortunately Spurs hadn't read the script – Blackburn won two-one at White Hart Lane. Now both City and Rovers each had a game to play. Blackburn had moved up to sixty-eight points, but with their goal difference an astonishing twenty-five goals greater than ours, they really had an extra point.

The build-up for my birthday was getting more nerve-wracking by the minute. I was asked what I wanted for my birthday. I only had one thing on my mind, and that was third place. Only the Norwich City players could provide that special birthday present. So the lads had an extra responsibility on their shoulders, though they didn't know it.

The night before the game I couldn't sleep, I was just so nervous about the game. We had played forty-one games and now it all came down to this one. The whole season had been amazing, and if I had a favourite season, this was it. We'd

Andy Johnson celebrates his goal in
the 3–3 draw at Ayresome Park

played with flair, passion, teamwork, and never knew when to give in. All the players gave their all that season, from goalie Bryan Gunn, player of the season and my all-time favourite player along with Darren Eadie, to Mark Robins up front, who scored so many important goals. Now they just had to do it one more time.

On the day I travelled up to Middlesbrough by coach with my friends Claire Gray, Suzanne, Katy and Grahame O'Regan. The journey was the longest of my life. I was getting more nervous by the minute, my birthday the last thing on my mind. I still couldn't get the game out of my head. We finally got to Ayresome Park. I was asked if I wanted to go for a beer before the game. It might have calmed the nerves, but no, I wanted to be in the ground.

There were plenty of Canaries fans to give Norwich their full support – two or three thousand. We were in full voice. 'On the ball, City' was being sung with passion, but out of superstition I refused to sing 'We're all going on a European tour'.

The game began. We were ninety minutes from success or failure.

Norwich started the game as they had all season, with all-out attacking play. No defending for a draw, that wasn't our style, we were going to try and win. It proved the right decision, when after thirteen minutes Bryan Gunn's long kick was flicked on by Efan Ekoku to Chris Sutton. Sutton laid it back to Ekoku, who shot. Boro keeper Andy Collett saved it, but the rebound again fell to Ekoku's feet.

Suddenly time slowed to a crawl. I remember anticipating Efan knocking the ball home. 'Go on, go on!' I shouted, like many other Norwich fans, and Ekoku duly obliged by smacking the ball home – one-nil. My hand was on Katy's shoulder, and as I jumped up in the air and surged forward, celebrating the goal, I took her with me without even knowing what I was doing. Fortunately, Claire got hold of her before she got hurt. 'Sorry Katy, I didn't realise what I was doing, I was too busy celebrating the goal.' Katy didn't care, and we started singing 'On the ball, City'.

Things continued to plan until the thirty-sixth minute, when John Hendrie crossed the ball over. Gunny came out but dropped the ball, and Willie Falconer smacked it home to make it one-all. It was still OK, Blackburn couldn't catch us if we drew. There were a couple more chances to both teams, but at half-time it remained one-one.

Blackburn were going to need at least two goals to overhaul us, but at Ewood Park it was goalless at half-time. Most Norwich fans were very confident; they were partying. I wasn't. I wouldn't celebrate until it was confirmed that Norwich were third. I didn't want to tempt fate.

The second half started. I remember Ruel Fox having a good chance to score, but his shot went wide. We were still hanging in there. Suddenly a goal at Ewood Park was announced on my radio. I stopped concentrating on the game in front of me. 'Blackburn have taken the lead through Tim Sherwood,' said the reporter. No, don't let an ex-Norwich player score the goal that ends my dreams. I was telling people what I had just heard. 'No worries, Spud,' people were telling me.

Then, thirty seconds later, came the kick in the stomach. A cross by Hendrie was met by a diving header by Paul Wilkinson and flew past Gunn. Two-one to Boro. I was too stunned to say anything. I was in shock – this can't be happening. Now Blackburn were third and we were fourth. We had been in the top three since the fifth game of the season, and here we were in the last game of the season, having worked so hard, and it was going to be taken away from us.

Norwich restarted the game and the ball went straight to Ruel Fox on the right wing. Foxy did a couple of shuffles and whipped a cross over, which was met by Sutton. The ball smacked the bar, but Ekoku was there for the rebound and headed home. Yeeessss! I went mad and surged forward to celebrate the goal, not dragging Katy with me this time, much to her relief. We were still singing and celebrating when Ian Crook received the ball in the middle of the park, chipped the ball forward to Andy Johnson, who burst through from midfield and the rifled a half-volley into the net. This time I didn't go mad. I just raised my arms aloft and shouted, 'Come on City, this time can you please hold onto it.' In five hectic minutes the scoring had gone one-nil Blackburn, two-one Middlesbrough and then three-two Norwich. Now surely we can't lose this, can we?

Within four minutes Boro's Hendrie played a one-two with Wilkinson, and from just outside the box shot passed Gunn into the bottom corner. Three-all. Norwich had a couple of chances to win it, but they went begging, and Boro had a spell when they had five consecutive corners, but luckily they came to nothing.

Today the fourth official tells you how much injury time there is when the game enters the ninetieth minute. Unfortunately back in 1993 that wasn't the case, so it was anyone's guess when the game would end. My watch told me we were in injury time, and I had just heard on the radio that the game at Ewood Park was over. Blackburn had won one-nil, so all we had to do was to hang on to a draw. I was staring at the referee, I didn't let him out of my sight, just praying for that final whistle, and eventually it arrived. Now it was party time! We were dancing around and singing. All the players came over to show their appreciation, the biggest cheers going up for manager Mike Walker and Player of the Year Bryan Gunn. We celebrated on the terraces for about thirty minutes, and the Middlesbrough stewards probably got fed up with us, but we had waited for this day for years and we weren't going to let anyone stop us from enjoying it. We then got on the coach for the journey home, and it was a happy one.

We stopped off at a pub on the way, and someone asked me if I was eighteen yet. I said, 'er, yes, by about an hour.' He said to the barmen, 'Right, get this man a beer, he's eighteen today and his team, Norwich, have just finished third in the Premier League.' About five people heard this as well and each of them got me a beer too. Suddenly I had half a dozen beers on the bar. I didn't have time to drink them all.

We finally got back into Norwich at 10.30pm, in time for Match of the Day. Unfortunately they only showed the goals, not the celebrations, but at least I could remember them. That day went down as the best day of my life. Today I tell people no-one could possibly have a better eighteenth birthday.

The following week Arsenal drew with Sheffield Wednesday in the FA Cup Final, but won the replay two-one, with ex-Canary Andy Linighan scoring the winner in the last minute. We were in Europe for the first time.

Fancy dress disaster

Middlesbrough 3–3 Norwich City ◌ Premier League ◌ 8 May 1993

By Peter Rogers

Peter is the Canaries' current Programme Editor, having joined the Club in this role in October 2000. Previously he worked for the Club on matchdays in the Canary Store from 1989 to 2000. He witnessed his first match at Carrow Road on April 4 1983, a 0–0 draw with arch rivals Ipswich Town.

The final match of the Canaries' 92/93 campaign away at Middlesbrough was a special one, both for the club and for me personally. A point from the game would guarantee Mike Walker's unfancied side a third-place finish in the Premier League and a possible venture into Europe the following season. For me, the game represented the end of a long but fantastic journey, as this was the first season that I had managed to watch every single Norwich game, home and away.

The season had been a real rollercoaster affair that included excellent wins at Highbury, Stamford Bridge and Villa Park. It had thrown in some tough times too, losing twice to Ipswich and a seven-one hammering at Blackburn. All in all the season was one that will live long in the memory, and it is no surprise that so many games from it feature in this book.

I'd used many modes of transport to get around the county following the fortunes of the eleven yellow wizards: car, minibus, train, plane and even Club Canary in times of desperation. For the final leg of this journey up to Teesside, a friend of mine with whom I went to most games that season, Rodney Charlwood, had got us booked on a minibus. The lads on the bus were made up of Rodney's building site workmates and stewards from Carrow Road.

Fans and players celebrate the Canaries' third place finish

A few days before the game Rodney did mention that a few of the lads on the minibus were going to the match in fancy dress, but personally he didn't fancy it. That was fine with me, as I've never been one for fancy dress. My fear of costumes goes back to my time at junior school – I attended the annual summer fête dressed as a Dalek, only to find there was no fancy dress that year! I've always feared that level of humiliation could resurface again whenever anyone mentions fancy dress, so I travelled in normal matchday attire. Big mistake. As Rodney and I joined the other lads on the bus we began to feel very uneasy in our trendy jeans and tee-shirts alongside Mickey Mouse, Pink Panther, a monk, a pirate, two convicts and about a dozen twelve-stone blokes dressed in blond wigs, stockings and suspenders.

Having come to terms with the embarrassment of being on the wrong end of a fancy dress situation once again, and laughed off the jokes about who I'd come dressed as, I knocked back a few cans and began to think about the big game ahead. The bus was full of lager-fuelled enthusiasm, as most were of the opinion that City would collect at least a point and secure third place. It would then be a case of supporting Arsenal in the FA Cup final against Sheffield Wednesday, since victory for the Gunners would hand the third-placed league side a place in the next season's UEFA Cup.

I must confess to being one of the Canaries' more pessimistic followers, and my record at Ayresome Park was mixed, having seen City there on two previous occasions. On my first visit I witnessed a real cracker. It was the first away match of 1988–89, and City ran out three-two winners in the August sunshine. I went with Rodney to that game too – a good omen. My second trip to Ayresome was a far less memorable affair, a two-nil defeat in the League Cup on a cold wet October night in 1990.

My big worry with this match was the fact that Boro were already relegated and had nothing to lose. Everyone else was trying to inform me that they'd gone down because they were rubbish, and we'd beat them no problem as their confidence and morale would be on the floor. But it wouldn't wash with me. I knew Norwich of old and feared the worst. Blackburn Rovers were the team chasing us for this all-important third place; they had an easy-looking fixture at home to Sheffield Wednesday.

Having parked up and whiled away an hour or so in a nice little drinking hole near to the ground, we made our way onto the terraces. The 2500-plus Norwich fans were housed in the East End of the ground in an open corner of terracing, the same corner I'd been on for the two-nil defeat in the League Cup back in 1990 – a bad sign, I thought.

The game was everything you don't want when you need a vital point – end-to-end, with chances coming and going for both teams. Fortunately it was City who took the lead, Efan Ekoku knocking the ball home at the second attempt. The goal, at our end of the ground, created delirium among the travelling fans. Boro were not to be denied though and hit back before the break with an effort from Willie Falconer.

With honours even at the break, it was time to listen out for what was happening at Ewood Park. The good news was that Blackburn were being held nil-nil in their quest to beat Sheffield Wednesday. As the second half started, even I felt reasonably confident that we'd make it, knowing that it would take goals in both games from Boro and Blackburn to halt the Canaries' charge to third place. Then my worst fears started to come true, as news that Blackburn were one up filtered around the Norwich fans. To make matters even worse – if that was remotely possible – the Blackburn goal had been scored by former Canary Tim Sherwood. Ex-players they never do you any favours do they?

Then my world came crashing down – Boro took a two-one lead through Paul Wilkinson. I was in a real state; I just couldn't come to terms with the fact that having been in the top three all season we were going to miss out at the death. Then if you ever needed proof that there is a God after all, we scored – not once but twice. First a Chris Sutton header hit the underside of the bar and Efan Ekoku was on hand to bundle home his second of the afternoon to send the Norwich fans absolutely mental. Then, just moments later, Andy Johnson burst through into the Boro penalty area and smashed us three-two up. The celebrations in that corner terrace were met with the same level of delight that greeted Steve Bruce's Milk Cup semi-final winner over a little-known club from somewhere north of Essex.

From hell to heaven at Ayresome Park, and it was still one-nil at Ewood Park. Of course Norwich, being Norwich, couldn't hold the lead, and gave us a pleasant wait for the final whistle. Boro got an equaliser and created a string of other opportunities before the referee called an end to the suffering on the away terrace and we could finally celebrate wining that vital point.

That third place was City's best ever league finish, and both the players and the fans celebrated in style at Ayresome Park and all the way back to Carrow Road. Of course, confirmation of the UEFA place depended on Arsenal winning the FA Cup the following weekend. The week's wait for the final was a long one, and not since 1978 have I ever wanted one team to win so badly, and Arsenal let us down then – not a good omen, I thought. After 120 minutes, with the score at one-all, you couldn't separate the two sides, and a replay was needed five days later. Just as in the first game, the match was all square at one-one and headed into extra-time. It looked as though for the first time in history the Cup Final would be decided by penalties – and more importantly, the Canaries' destiny was going to hinge on spot kicks that they themselves had no control over. But then – deep, deep into injury time of extra time – Andy Linighan popped up to head home the winner and send the Canaries flying into Europe. Now what was that I was saying about ex-players never doing you any favours!

Lifting the hoodoo

Sheffield Wednesday 3–3 Norwich City ● FA Carling Premiership ●
1 September 1993

By Sharon Butcher

Sharon's love of Norwich City has overcome many obstacles: starting life as a West Bromwich fan, witnessing a defeat at the hands of Ipswich at her very first match and even being banned from fixtures by her husband to be. However, Sharon persevered an now leads a committed Canaries posse.

Let's get one thing clear. I was a West Brom fan when I met my husband-to-be. I'd never seen Norwich City. I didn't even know they played in yellow and green, though I soon did when I first entered his home. The Baggies were still my lot – my father supported them, and one of my earliest childhood memories is him driving us past the Hawthorns in his lorry and delivering an ear-shattering blast of the horn to alert the sleeping stadium to our presence.

But I did say 'was' a Baggies fan. For in 1992 I had got to know Rob, handsome and intelligent and the most dedicated, loyal, passionate and loving man I have ever met. Trouble was, Norwich City were the subject of his strongest affections, as I'd soon discover. And so, in order to be closer to the man of my dreams, I changed allegiance and a Canary follower I became. I discarded the stripy scarves and invested in a green and yellow version instead.

Initially he was reluctant to take me. He thought his team wouldn't approve of the new love in his life, but eventually he succumbed and I donned the colours for the first time.

After my first visit, Rob was not best pleased. Livid in fact. We lost two-nil to the unmentionable team from Suffolk. But that one wasn't my fault – he blamed the Sky Strikers, who'd distracted the team on the pitch before the game, he reckoned. But then we lost the next two games he took me to by the same scoreline. And that's when I got it in the neck.

He banned me and declared a five-mile exclusion zone round Carrow Road where I was forbidden to set foot. Off he went, alone again, to Carrow Road, whereupon they promptly won. Point proved, he said.

I resigned myself to never going again, but one day I got the bug again. Realising that Rob would never entertain the prospect of me joining him for a match, a friend and I surreptitiously took a vehicle up to Hillsborough for an evening match. Avoiding my husband for the evening, we took our places at the back of the stand and settled down for the match, dreading the outcome. As he would no doubt have done himself, had he known I was there.

The whistle blew to begin the game. Wednesday had ex-Norwich and England keeper Chris Woods in goal, Chris Waddle on the wing and other classy players

Mark Bowen's goal at Hillsborough set the Canaries up for a wonderful comeback

like Andy Sinton in the side. City had plenty of talent of their own though: Bryan Gunn in sticks, a solid back four with Bowen and Culverhouse, Ian Crook in midfield, Foxy on the wing and Chris Sutton up front.

The game looked evenly matched, and my chances of ending the jinx looked good. But when Wednesday took a two-goal lead my heart sank. I held my head in my hands. So did Rob. Then he booted the seat in front of him in frustration and marched off to find some refreshment. He looked in a right strop. When he returned they were three up – his tea went over the edge of the upper tier. I was almost relieved that I couldn't be blamed for the same scoreline yet again.

'Waddle for England', sang the Owls' supporters. Jolly right too I thought – good-looking chap. 'Sinton for England', they continued, suggesting their judgement of talent wasn't so sound after all.

With twenty minutes left, I saw something that I thought I'd never see – a Norwich City goal. And what a splendid one it was too, as Mark Bowen rifled a rising drive in to the top of the net from way outside the area. I was then treated to a demonstration of Rob's 'raison d'être'. Polite applause ensued from the Wednesday fans, who obviously had this down as a consolation strike, but even at three-nil down, with no apparent way back, my man and his mates were going ballistic, clenching their fists and roaring encouragement.

As an understanding of his ways began to dawn on me, so did the prospect of an unlikely result from a hopeless-looking situation, as Efan Ekoku converted a Ruel Fox cross at the near post to reduce the deficit to a single goal. Cue pandemonium among the City fans, silence across the way.

And as Chris Sutton, one of City's greatest sons, coolly slotted home the third past former City keeper Chris Woods, all hell literally broke loose. Sutton roared his delight. Gunny clenched his fists and shook his golden locks before the City fans and in one joyous bundle of celebration my hubby-to-be emerged with a huge grin on his face and his hands clasped towards the sky in mock gratitude. I was celebrating with my friend in much the same way.

On the final whistle, as the City team acknowledged the support of those Canary fans who had made the trek, I announced my presence to my startled partner. It took him a while to take it in – all of two or three seconds to be precise, then he returned to celebrate with his mates.

My goalscoring duck had been broken, and even if I hadn't seen City win yet, the hoodoo my man had assumed was down to me had been lifted and I was allowed to return to the home of football itself, albeit on probation. But at least City won that time!

70

The Midfield General

Norwich City 3–0 Vitesse Arnhem ⚽ UEFA Cup first round, first leg ⚽ 15 September 1993

By Dave Major

Dave became a regular at Carrow Road in the 1989/90 season when Norwich City were languishing in the middle of Division One.

Norwich City's European adventures are generally remembered for moments of brilliance – Jerry Goss's goal in Munich, Bryan Gunn's save from Adolfo Valencia, the gallant battle in Milan. But one game and one performance rates as highly in my memory as any of the above – Norwich's first game in Europe against Vitesse Arnhem, and the performance of one Gary Megson.

Now, the name Gary Megson is not one you would expect to see in a book of such memories. 'Wasn't he the manager who tried to take us down in two successive seasons? Robert Chase's final mouthpiece?' Well, while we can scoff at his management, his exploits on the field in this victory and his general combative nature provided the catalyst for a victorious run.

In many ways, Megson personified the Norwich City team of the day, full of players who had worked their way up from lower leagues and reserve team football to play on the finest stage in Europe. The captains in these games – John Polston, Ian Butterworth and Rob Newman among others – could surely have only dreamed of playing on such a stage just a few years earlier.

Norwich City had had to wait for European football for eight years. Three times before they had been denied: the Milk Cup final winners and the teams of 1986/87 and 1988/89 would all have qualified for Europe had English teams not been banned after the Heysel disaster. It was something that Norwich had had to wait for – and an opportunity they would not let slip through their fingers now.

Gary Megson and Arnhem's skipper Theo Bos exchange views during the Canaries' European debut

The first half went mainly to plan – the fifteenth seeds in the UEFA cup made the running and gave Norwich an education in European football. But around halfway through the half came what I feel was the major turning point of the tie. The dangerous Glenn Helder, later to join Arsenal, danced down the left wing, and across came Megson who caught him with his second leg after missing him with the first. It was one of those challenges that Megson is often remembered for, and he was rightly booked for it. Minutes, a similar robust but fair challenge sent Efan Ekoku away on a run. It was a clear sign that Norwich were wrestling control of the midfield battleground, with Megson leading the way.

All of a sudden Norwich threatened more as an attacking outfit and Megson was everywhere. Headed clearances from the Vitesse defence seemed magnetically drawn to him, and he was at the heart of everything Norwich put together. But despite these best efforts, at the break it was nil-nil.

The second half could have been so different. Two minutes before Norwich scored, a cross from the right was missed by John Polston and the Vitesse forward had two stabs at the ball before it ran out of play. After that let-off, Norwich went up to the other end and after prolonged pressure through midfield, Efan Ekoku scored the first goal. An exquisite Ian Crook chip found him on the right-hand side of the River End box, and he finished on the volley into the bottom left-hand corner. A brilliant goal!

Norwich, lifted by the goal, were then indebted to their goalkeeper. Bryan Gunn, who would go on to make heroic saves in all of Norwich's European games, saved a rasping drive from Glenn Helder when his pace had taken him away from the Norwich defence. It was a warning sign that Vitesse were not yet beaten, although their attacking forays were becoming more sporadic.

But it was the pace and the passion driven through midfield that pushed Norwich on: the subtlety of Ian Crook's passing, the forward running of Jerry Goss, and the passion and drive of Gary Megson.

The second goal involved all three elements. Crook was released on the right-hand side of the area. His cross was missed by Megson on the edge of the six-yard box but not by Goss, standing on the penalty spot, who swivelled and shot into the bottom left hand corner. Not as spectacular as those volleys, but so important to the cause.

Vitesse now looked beaten. The pace and passion that Norwich had injected into the game during the second half was something they were clearly not used to in the Dutch League. Panic had set in within the defence, and when Vitesse failed to clear a corner, a cross from the right was deflected into the path of John Polston, captain for the day, and Norwich were in dreamland – three-nil.

When Megson walked from the pitch with around ten minutes to go, he left to a standing ovation – a near-capacity crowd recognising his personal contribution to the victory. His departure signalled the start of a glittering Norwich City career for one Darren Eadie, the eighteen-year-old who would star for Norwich during a difficult period for the club. Eadie's first contribution was a dazzling seventy-yard run and cross that just evaded the onrushing Sutton. A sign of so many things to come.

The game finished three-nil – an emphatic start to the European adventure. As I look back, my lasting memory of the game is of Megson's standing ovation. If anyone is in any doubt as to the impact that Megson had on Norwich from a playing perspective, pull out the video of this game and enjoy!

71

Into the unknown

Vitesse Arnhem 0–0 Norwich City ☾ UEFA Cup first round, second leg ☾ 29 September 1993

By Kathy Blake

The veteran of 35 years of Canary campaigns here remembers her first taste of European competition.

It may seem strange to choose a nil-nil draw as one of the most memorable matches you have attended, but this one holds a special place in my affections for two reasons. Firstly, it was a journey into the unknown: City had never set foot on foreign soil in meaningful matches before. Also, I came very close to missing it altogether. Like all travelling fans, I had been issued with a reservation slip a week earlier with a departure time of 4.30am on it. In the meantime, the club had brought this forward to 2.30am, and I had somehow managed not to spot this in the local press. Consequently I arrived at Carrow Road at 4am to find

Chris Sutton takes a tumble in the second leg of the Arnhem tie

the place shrouded in darkness. A sense of foreboding came over me and a brief conversation with one of the remaining policemen confirmed my worst fears. The coaches had long gone. I was absolutely gutted, as I had been waiting for that day since I'd first started following City.

All of a sudden, a car came screeching into the car park. I went over to the driver to discover he had done exactly the same thing. 'Shall we go for it?' he said. I didn't need a second invitation, and jumped into his car. I had never met the chap before, didn't know his name and have not set eyes on him since, but he drove flat out and we finally caught the coaches up at Dover services. We hopped on board and had a reasonably calm channel crossing, finally arriving in the historic town of Arnhem about 4pm. It was a strange, almost unreal experience supporting Norwich abroad along with so many other City fans. The ground was a bit like Carrow Road twenty-five years ago. The police seemed to be on high alert, with English fans in town, but ended up looking faintly puzzled by these good-natured fans in yellow and green.

The match was a low-key affair. Vitesse never looked like threatening the three-goal lead we had from the first leg, and City – in their unfamiliar navy away strip – almost nicked it right at the end.

We arrived back in Norwich at 10am. I hadn't slept for fifty hours but I was very happy. I went straight into work, where my colleagues sat me in a corner and left me alone for the rest of the day!

72

Making history

Vitesse Arnhem 0–0 Norwich City ⟲ UEFA Cup first round, second leg ⟲ 29 September 1993

By Steve Smith

Steve has been a supporter since 1981 but confesses his first vivid memories are of a Youth Cup Final against Everton in the early '80s.

In autumn 1993 I was finishing my final year at Norwich City College, which coincided with Norwich having their best ever season in the top flight. I remember a group of us making our way up to Middlesborough, singing our heads off and watching a three-three draw that, coupled with the Blackburn result, meant we had a fighting chance of getting into Europe. It all hinged on Arsenal doing a cup double, but that was utterly irrelevant for those supporters in Middlesborough – once we knew we were in third place the only song that could be heard was 'We're all going on a European tour'…

Ten days later, Andy Linighan's last-gasp header won the cup for Arsenal and suddenly the dream was reality – we were in the UEFA Cup. I will never ever forget that crazy night.

Unfortunately for me, finishing college meant a new job that took me to Brighton. I can remember starting work there at the end of July '93, eager to impress because I needed three days off in September to watch our first ever European away game. The day arrived and I boarded the coach to take me from Brighton to London and then on to Norwich. The excitement of that first trip meant that I got no sleep during the evening. We met at Carrow Road around midnight, in a car park full of nervous supporters, not quite knowing what to expect. Twenty-four coaches were lined up ready to go; we were in the middle batch of eight that left around 1am and made its way down to the Dover ferry. I can remember it being pretty dark, making our way from the coach up to the restaurant on the ferry. Once in the restaurant it was a different

Fans celebrate the Canaries gaining a place in the second round of the UEFA Cup

story. The entire place was like being in the club shop – it was just a sea of yellow and green, all of us tucking into fried breakfasts, reading the morning papers and hoping for the best.

We made our way through France and into Belgium, occasionally bursting into song at the odd amusing sight, before disembarking at a roadside café. The first eight coaches had just left; the poor bloke in charge didn't know what had just hit him as another 400 supporters came in and cleared him out of food and drink. The slight smile he wore as we left changed to a look of absolute horror as yet another eight coaches pulled in!

We continued on our journey and arrived in Arnhem in the early afternoon. As we got off the coaches, we just followed the trail of yellow and green as it made for a shopping precinct that had a few shops and several pubs. It had, as expected, been taken over by our supporters and as we sat there the number of fans grew and grew. By now the singing was in full swing, every football song I had ever learnt was being sung and obviously being three-nil up from the first leg meant we were quite hopeful.

We made for the ground, could not believe it when it turned out to be in the middle of a forest, and made our way through the barbed-wire fences to the worst away section I have ever been to – steep, uneven concrete with grass growing through it everywhere.

It was a carnival atmosphere throughout the game. The players were cheered non-stop, although the game itself does not live in the memory as a classic. I remember Efan Ekoku continually tripping over the ball, and Gunny making the odd save, but we were never really in danger and it ended nil-nil. After the match was over we just kept singing before getting back on to the coaches and heading back to Calais. The journey back was a bit quieter. Reading the following morning's papers had a sobering effect, as they didn't seem to share the elation that I had felt the night before.

The coaches plodded back to Norwich and arrived at 11am. For me, adrenalin had given way to tiredness as the realisation dawned that I had another six hours on two more coaches back to Brighton ahead of me.

I will always remember getting back to my hotel at 7.30pm to be greeted by two members of staff who wanted to know how my three days away were. Was Holland nice? What was the weather like? they asked. They had no idea that I had experienced my beloved football team getting through to the next round of the UEFA Cup to face a team called Bayern Munich. I couldn't make that game, but was comforted in the knowledge that we had made a bit of history.

73

Euro heroes

Bayern Munich 1–2 Norwich City ⚽ UEFA Cup second round, first leg ⚽ 20 October 1993

By Kevin Piper

Kevin Piper is Anglia Television's Sports Editor and in that position he has to maintain total impartiality when it comes to presenting football coverage in the Anglia region. When asked, he states that Halifax Town are his favourite team, but for a Norwich lad, brought up on the exploits of Keelan, Bryceland, Foggo and Crickmore in the 1960s, it is not difficult to work out where his loyalties lie.

I can remember my first ever game. I came to Carrow Road especially to see Kevin Keelan play, only to find that Peter Vasper had taken his place. At school we always used to have to write about what we did each weekend, so my stories always revolved around Norwich City matches.

I didn't have to dig too deep for my most memorable Norwich City match. I would like to be able to pick out some obscure match that was singularly memorable for me, but in all honesty I cannot overlook the Canaries' victory in Munich.

With all due respect, very few people expected Norwich to win at such an historic stadium against a team full of world-class players, but they did! Everything about that night was memorable. The sense of occasion, the setting, the atmosphere and obviously the result. In fact, when Mark Bowen made it two-nil, I was moved to ring my wife from the stadium to make sure the score was the same on the television!

Despite Bayern's attempts at a comeback, the resilient Canaries held on to record an historic victory.

The second half was not one of the classiest Norwich performances I have seen, but it was full of character and to be there, in any capacity, was tremendous.

Kevin visits the Olympic Stadium prior to the match

74

Playing in Europe

Norwich City 1–1 Bayern Munich ☾ UEFA Cup ☾ second round, second leg ☾ 3 November 1993

By Ian Butterworth

Ian played in 286 matches for the Canaries, making his debut on 20 September 1986 in an away fixture with Aston Villa. Since leaving the Club Ian has taken his considerable talent into management and is currently head coach at Cardiff City.

Playing in European football is every player's ambition. In my time at Carrow Road we had qualified for a UEFA Cup place twice before, only to be prevented from taking our rightful place by the ban on English clubs at that time. When we finally took our place, the tie against Vitesse Arnhem gave us a taste of what it was all about.

Not surprisingly, the game at Bayern's Olympic Stadium is also high on my list. The achievement of winning there against a team including some world-class players will stand for evermore. Having taken a two-nil lead we then defended it brilliantly, despite their goal just before half-time. It was a tremendous team performance, and although the stadium was less than full, it was a great occasion.

For the second leg at Carrow Road, expectations were high and eventually fulfilled. The build-up within the city leading up to the match was fantastic, everyone was keyed up for the game itself. The atmosphere inside the ground was the best I have ever known it, with the crowd lifting us to greater efforts.

Bayern's early goal was a setback, but we always felt confident and remained composed, eventually equalising to see us through three-two on aggregate. The celebrations immediately after the game were an expression of our delight in beating such a mighty club over a two-legged European tie.

Ian on the lap of honour after helping defeat the mighty Germans

75

End of a European adventure

Internazionale 1–0 Norwich City ⚽ UEFA Cup third round, second leg ⚽ 8 December 1993

By Steve Trivett

Steve attended his first Norwich City match at the tender age of three and a year later witnessed the Milk Cup triumph at Wembley. In over 21 years of supporting the Club his memories include close encounters of the friendly kind with Sunderland supporters and playing a three-hour football match at Calais.

What is my outstanding memory from twenty-one years of supporting City? I can't remember much about my early matches, although I understand that I was already showing a disregard for authority at the age of three, when at Notts County I fed sweets to a police dog before marching off with a parking cone. I was at Wembley when we won the Milk Cup, but my memories are a bit sketchy as I was only four, although I've been told I shook hands with loads of Sunderland fans and was even picked up and kissed by a couple of hefty Wearsiders! The near-double season of 1988/89 had some great matches, and I do remember jumping around the Millwall terrace after Robert Fleck's late winner, totally oblivious to the hostile stares across the fence. You don't see fear when you're seven. The season we finished third was just one long great memory, although the comeback at Arsenal stands out. More recently there have been a couple of great wins at Ipswich. However I think City's away match at Inter Milan is my outstanding memory.

I'd always been promised that I could go to City's first match in Europe, and I really enjoyed our visit to Arnhem. My parents decreed I should go to school while they swanned off to Munich, but when the draw for City to visit mighty Inter Milan was made I wasn't being left behind. A quick call to school elicited the remark that I'd learn more in two days going to Milan than I would at school – I don't know whether that reflected on the teaching at Stalham High or my own attitude to schoolwork!

The coach left Norwich on Tuesday morning, and twenty-four long hours later we arrived in misty Milan. Over three thousand City fans had made the trip and the atmosphere was brilliant. As the stadium towered above us I couldn't believe my team was playing there. Despite being a goal down from the first leg and losing six or seven players to injury and suspension, Norwich outplayed their famous hosts, only bad luck and poor finishing preventing them from recording a historic win. The fans never stopped singing encouragement to the team as they laid siege to the Inter goal, but in the end a breakaway goal from Dennis Bergkamp put an end to City's European tour.

At the end, the Norwich fans sang 'Mike Walker's yellow and green army' for

Gary Megson in the thick of the action against Inter

about forty-five minutes as the Inter coach and Milan police looked on in utter amazement. Many fans say this is their main memory of the trip; mine, however seems to be from about eighteen hours later.

After an all-night trip with me asleep in the aisle of the coach (I was the youngest and so got away with it), we arrived at Calais to find all ferries delayed by storm-force winds. So what did forty or fifty fans who had been travelling for the best part of forty-eight hours do? We played a three-hour football match! The result? My team won, with Angela Shipley scoring at least two goals.

As we arrived back in Norwich, some fifty-six hours after setting out, we were all optimistically looking forward to returning to Europe. I still am!

76

Devoted fans salute European heroes

Internazionale 1–0 Norwich City ◌ UEFA Cup ◌ 8 December 1993

By Graeme Davies

Graeme first saw Norwich play against Orient in a pre-season friendly match at Carrow Road on 7 August 1976.

A few years ago the BBC released a series of highlights videos for a number of clubs, including one for Norwich. Right at the start, John Motson describes our victory over Bayern Munich as the club's greatest ever night. I was there that night, and excellent though it was, I take issue with that choice on two grounds. For the overwhelming majority of City fans, the 1985 Milk Cup semi-final victory over that team beginning with 'I' will always be our best ever. And secondly, Bayern wasn't even the high point of our 1993 UEFA Cup run. In fact, the finest moment of the story came about half an hour after we'd been knocked out.

This might come as a shock to many Manchester United fans, but sometimes it's more glorious to fail. And so it was with our foray into Europe. The visit to Vitesse Arnhem was an adventure, but we'd already won the tie in the first leg at Carrow Road. Munich, when people took photos of the scoreboard in disbelief, was unforgettable. But only after we'd lost in the San Siro did it all really sink in, and the response from the 3000 Norwich fans there was superb.

For most of our travelling support, the journey to Milan was quick and easy, because they travelled by 'plane. For those who, for financial reasons, travelled on the four coaches that took the road route to Italy, it wasn't the most pleasant trip – in contrast with earlier rounds.

The previous coach trips – to Holland and Germany – had been quite good fun, if a little cramped. Club Canary's coach stewards had managed the trips in their usual friendly, laid-back manner. We'd won over the local police in Belgium, Holland and Germany, who soon realised that we were not going to go on the rampage. Their original plans had required us to be kept in holding areas (actually barren industrial wastegrounds) for several hours. Unfortunately, our good reputation didn't seem to have reached the police and immigration officials at the Franco-Italian border. They stopped us for nearly an hour and hand-searched every bag. The sense of frustration after the long drive through France was tangible.

We eventually arrived in Milan about an hour before the game, meeting up with those who had flown. From far away you could hear the noise from our allocated corner of the ground; apparently the early arrivals had begun singing about an hour before that. No-one in the Norwich corner would fall silent for another three hours.

From outside the San Siro stadium is simply magnificent. The four familiar spiral-towered corners are visible for miles, and the impressive architecture tells you you're about to see something special. Inside, though, the facilities were disappointing and the condition of the pitch was far from perfect – big stadia always have this problem, as shadows from large stands stop sunlight from reaching the grass.

I've often wondered how Manchester United became the richest club in the world when there are other, bigger clubs like Inter, AC Milan and Barcelona who could easily compete. But United sell merchandise almost everywhere, while neither of the Milan teams have club shops at their own grounds, relying instead on privately run stalls on their concourse.

As the waiting went on we passed the time away singing. 'On the ball, City' rang out repeatedly, and I don't think the sparsely spread Inter fans could quite understand what these strange English fans were getting so worked up about when nothing was going on.

Rob Newman crunches into a tackle in the San Siro

Then came the game, accompanied by continuous song from the Norwich corner. We were one down after the home leg, and had several players suspended, including our playmaker Ian Crook. There was no reason to be optimistic about our chances of overturning a deficit against one of European football's biggest names, but such was the nature of Mike Walker's first spell in charge that we were beginning to feel that nothing was impossible, especially after Munich. More importantly, the players felt the same. Roared on by the travelling 'yellow army', they simply tore into our hosts. Sutton and Ekoku wasted four or five gilt-edged chances to get us level, as the whole game was played out at speed immediately in front of us. Football folklore is full of 'if onlys', and here was ours. If we'd just taken one of those first-half opportunities, Inter would have collapsed and we'd have added another massive name to our giant-killing history. Moreover, we would have gone on to play the only other decent team left in the competition, Borussia Dortmund. Having overcome them, we would probably have won the whole competition. If only…

We didn't score, and after the break the Italians were, well, Italian. We had plenty of possession but Inter effectively killed the game off. The only incident I remember at all in the second half was Dennis Bergkamp's injury-time winner. It was a class finish from a class player, who unfortunately has scored every time he's played against Norwich. You'd think he'd be a bit more generous, given that he spent his childhood family holidays touring near Carrow Road!

That was it, our run was over, but we still hadn't reached the defining moment that made this such a special occasion. Throats aching from several hours' continual chanting, we still kept on. On and on and on and on. The departing Italians turned back and came back to applaud us, watching in awe as we sang 'Mike Walker's green and yellow army' over and over again. Even the sour-faced police applauded , although they drew the line at swapping their riot helmets for our beanie hats!

For half an hour, we got louder and louder still. Then came the moment. Walker came out to do a television interview and the place just erupted, bursting into the loudest rendition of 'On the ball, City' I've ever heard – and I've heard it more than once or twice. At that moment you just knew you were experiencing something unique, and I think many of us subconsciously realised it would never be so good again. It was a moment that perfectly summed up the sheer emotion that football can generate, and why millions of people around the world care so much about the game. It brought a lump to the throat, but the tears were tears of pride. Sometimes you win even when you lose.

77

Mike Walker's yellow and green army

Tottenham Hotspur 1–3 Norwich City ⚽ Premier League ⚽ 27 December 1993

By Keith Newton

Canary enthusiast, Keith Newton, recalls fond memories of a 3–1 win at White Hart Lane in the Canaries' 1993/94 Premiership campaign.

It was just after Christmas. I had persuaded my little sister that she wanted an away trip to Tottenham as a birthday present. It was to be her first Norwich game.

We nearly failed to get tickets on the day, such was the crowd, but we just got in. We had only just gone out of Europe, and the Norwich crowd was full of talk of the San Siro. This, combined with the sold-out crowd of 33,130 filling White Hart Lane, created a good-humoured match day atmosphere. Mike Walker was in charge (shortly to go to Everton) and we still had that team in place.

The match started, and we were in full voice watching the passing game that had made Norwich so successful over the last few years. A just reward soon came: Ekoku got one, then Sutton got another to give us a comfortable lead at half-time. Everything was going to plan.

Visiting the gents at half-time, I could see some locked-out Spurs fans out of the window. They couldn't resist aiming some friendly taunts at the Norwich contingent – it was great to be able to gesture the score back.

The second half started and Nicky Barmby quickly pulled one back, worrying us a bit. But such was the feeling of confidence in those days that it only served to bring on a continuous chorus of 'Mike Walker's yellow and green army' for what seemed like the rest of the game. We played well and finally got the third goal we deserved. Ekoku received it on the right, heading towards us, cut in and rather selfishly blasted straight at the keeper when it would have been better to square it to Chris Sutton. The goalie blocked well, but it fell to Sutton anyway, and he knocked in the simple ball.

We all went mad until the final whistle. All I could hear as we walked out of the ground was: 'Jingle bells, jingle bells, jingle all the way, Oh what fun it is to see Norwich win away!'

Chris Sutton scored three goals against Spurs in 1993/94 including two in a 3–1 win at White Hart Lane

78

Norwich spoil a Kop party

Liverpool 0–1 Norwich City ☾ Premier League ☾ 30 April 1994

By Daniel Kinsman

When Daniel first saw Norwich City play against Tottenham on 16 October 1982 the 0–0 score may not have been too exciting, but the Canaries line-up included some great names in the Club's history – Chris Woods, Martin O'Neill, John Deehan and Keith Bertschin.

One of my most memorable Norwich matches was the second from last league game of the 1993/94 season, away to Liverpool. Norwich were disappointingly placed mid-table in the Premier League, having challenged and finished third the previous season, and consequently competed in the UEFA Cup. This was the season Mike Walker left to manage Everton, leaving John Deehan in charge. Ruel Fox had also left, but for the time being we were hanging on to striker Chris Sutton.

At the time of the match I was a student at Bangor University in North Wales, only a relatively short hop from Merseyside. I was a member of the college hockey club and, as luck would have it, two of my fellow players turned out to be Canaries fans! Having had to watch the European games on television or listen on the radio, we decided the away trip to Liverpool was the perfect time to see the team play again. Student grants didn't exactly stretch to football tickets but we felt it a worthy cause!

The day arrived and brought a respite from the North Wales rain; the sun was actually shining in a blue sky – a good omen! Liverpool were seventh in the table, with nothing to play for, but the significance of the game was that it would be the last time the famous Kop stand would be used before being pulled down in the summer.

The train took us along the Welsh coastline and over the border to Chester, where we picked up the Metro train into Liverpool. We had some time to kill before the match so we soaked up some pre-match atmosphere in the city and marvelled at the array of shellsuit-wearing Scousers! As match time approached, we boarded a bus from the city centre that we hoped was going near the ground. The bus departed crammed with Liverpool fans, so we guessed we were on the right track. We didn't take too much grief from them – beating Bayern Munich earlier in the season demanded respect!

By now the atmosphere was terrific. The game was a 44,000 sell-out, and the last few streets on the way to Anfield were buzzing. At the ground, which none of us had previously visited, we passed through the famous iron gates with their 'You'll never walk alone' motto and found our seats in the Anfield Road stand. We were in the front row of a block of Norwich fans, looking directly down the pitch to the Kop. The Liverpool supporters had taken to the terraces early and the Kop was a dazzling red mass of scarves, flags and banners.

As kick-off approached we were presented with entertainment in honour of the occasion. To great appreciation (mostly from the home fans) we were introduced to a string of Anfield legends including Emlyn Hughes, Steve Heighway, Ray Clemence and Kenny Dalglish. Finally we were treated to a rendition of 'You'll Never Walk Alone' by Gerry Marsden and the Liverpool Philharmonic Community Choir.

At last three o'clock was upon us and the teams took to the pitch. The City line-up included Gunn, Sutton, Ekoku, Crook, Bowen and Goss. Liverpool fielded a mixture of youth and experience; the familiar faces of John Barnes and Ian Rush survived alongside the youngsters Fowler, Redknapp and McManaman.

Norwich enjoyed most of the possession thanks to Crook and Goss in the midfield. Attacking the Kop end in the first half, we all hoped that City would go into the record books for scoring the last goal at this end. The dream looked like coming true as the ball broke for Jerry Goss on the edge of the Liverpool penalty area. He unleashed a curling shot with the outside of his right foot that was destined for the top corner of David James' goal. Before the ball hit the net we were jumping in the air in celebration. What a beauty! One-nil – the Kop was silent and all we had to do now was keep a clean sheet!

Gossy is mobbed having silenced the Kop

As it turned out, Norwich had the best chances in the second half. We had a few tense moments before the final whistle, but in the end Norwich spoilt the Kop party with an excellent end-of-season win.

It was a good feeling travelling home in the early evening sunshine having seen our team win away, then heading straight for the Student Union bar for a few celebratory pints! Although I have nothing but good memories of this particular match, it is still a nightmare to think that even after playing against the likes of Liverpool, Manchester United and Bayern Munich we were still relegated the next season. The only consolation was that Ipswich came with us!

79

Norwich–Liverpool through the years

30 June 1994

By Sandra Fishwick

Sandra, a schoolteacher and prototype 'ladette', has been attending Canaries matches since 1972, when she first discovered the the joys of mid-winter at the old River End terrace and warming up with a few pints and a bout of post-match analysis.

Fixtures against the mighty Liverpool are some of the most memorable of my thirty years as a City fan. Not only were there some tremendous individual performances, but they also catalogue a lifetime of football experiences! It is impossible to pick one game out of the many stirring encounters that I can remember, so I would like to summarise six Norwich–Liverpool games that have particular significance for me.

Norwich–Liverpool in 1978 was my first match at Carrow Road since returning from college. I hadn't seen City for many months, though my grandmother would send me the Pink Un each week – this was regarded as rather strange! The last time I had seen City was away at a very muddy Baseball Ground, when I had been the only one cheering as Duncan Forbes scored a rare goal. This Liverpool game was rather less memorable: we lost, and my memories are mainly of how cold it was in the old River End.

Norwich–Liverpool in 1980 was of course the famous game that Liverpool won five-three, Justin Fashanu scoring the Goal of the Season with a tremendous volley. David Fairclough, later to play briefly for City, scored a hat-trick. It was probably one of the most exiting games ever seen at Carrow Road. I couldn't see a thing from the middle of the Barclay, but what an atmosphere!

Liverpool–Norwich in 1983 took place during the season I discovered away matches. I went to quite a few, including the infamous cup match at Brighton. It was a real thrill for me to go to Anfield. At that time Liverpool were in a class of their own and rarely lost at all, never mind at home. City obviously hadn't read the script, as the game was notable for a Mark Lawrenson own goal and a fantastic strike from Martin O'Neill. Strangely enough, there was a complete lack of the famous Scouse wit at the ground, though we all laughed…

In the eighties I was something of a ladette, long before the term was ever invented. I loved having a few pints and going to the football. I had one particular mate with whom I went to most matches, and we would routinely celebrate or drown our sorrows after the game. Before Norwich–Liverpool in 1987 I was so sure City would win that I put some champagne on ice at home, and sure enough they did. It was the first league game in which Ian Rush scored, but Liverpool still lost. Let's just say that my life changed that night, thanks to our two-one win.

1994

The Canaries upset Liverpool's party for the last game in front of a terraced Kop in April 1994

Robert Fleck, my all-time Norwich hero, scored some wonderful goals for City – the hat-trick against Sutton United and his marvellous volley in the televised game at Millwall spring to mind. I have no recollection of the date of this Liverpool game, but I remember I was sitting in the South Stand. We were already winning two-nil. Flecky received the ball from the half-way line just in front of me and, in a move that Ryan Giggs would emulate years later, passed several international defenders with ease (Alan Hansen take note) and cut inside the penalty area to score with a powerful shot. Sheer class.

I was lucky enough to be a guest in the Bob Paisley lounge on the day that Liverpool played their final game in front of the old Kop in 1994. Famous Reds from the past waved to the crowd, and the widows of Shankly and Paisley were also there. There was a real carnival atmosphere. Everyone was very kind to the only City fan in the Centenary Stand, but they assured me that Norwich had no chance. Imagine their surprise when Gossy scored a typical wonder goal, the only goal of the game, in front of that famous stand. Though the Reds may disagree, it was a fitting goal to mark the occasion. Liverpool fans were magnanimous in their appreciation of this and it was a good day to be a Norwich fan.

All these games shine bright in my memory. Football is a kind of drug and certain matches just stay with you long after the final whistle – you long for another fix of such incredible excitement. Nothing beats the thrill of winning, and if your team can do it with style and panache, as City so often have, then so much the better. I look forward to the day when, once again, we not only play teams like Liverpool on a regular basis, but also have the audacity to humiliate them from time to time.

There is a postscript to all this. Through watching Norwich I now have more than a passing interest in Liverpool's progress, as I ended up marrying my aforementioned friend. Originally a Reds supporter, he is now also a City season ticket holder along with his wife. When we married we had a wedding cake with both team crests as decoration. Now how strange is that?

80

Having fondly remembered the thrill of UEFA competition, Dave has a second shot at describing a great moment for Norwich City.

The record signing – Jon Newsome

By Dave Major

'If fifty per cent of your transfers are a success, you're doing well.' This ratio is well applied to the transfer dealings of many recent Norwich City managers. We've had our fair share of duff transfers, especially over the last few years – step forward Steve Walsh, Kevin Scott and Raymond de Waard. But we can also point to some very good transfer business by many Norwich City managers – Iwan Roberts signing from Wolves, Gary Holt from Kilmarnock and Mark Robins from Manchester United, to name but a few.

But one signing will stand out from the others, and it shouldn't just be because for the last eight years it's featured in the Norwich City records as the highest transfer fee paid for a player. It was June 1994 when Norwich finally paid seven figures for an individual, despite having received more than a million for many players before. The player was Jon Newsome, a commanding central defender from Premiership rivals Leeds United. He was to star in an extremely difficult time for the club.

Newsome had been tracked for a while by the previous management team of Mike Walker and John Deehan. When Deehan succeeded Walker as manager, his first significant close season capture was Newsome, who he immediately installed as Club captain in the absence of previous skipper Ian Butterworth, out with what proved to be a career-ending injury.

1994

Six months had passed since Norwich had been eliminated from the UEFA cup after a gallant fight in Milan. Since then management had changed, key players departed, and City's Achilles' heel, its defence, was leaking alarmingly. Dreadful defensive displays at home to QPR and Southampton the previous season had only emphasised that it needed improvement. Newsome was signed with Carl Bradshaw and Mike Milligan to add some much-needed steel and cover for a shaky defence.

Jon Newsome still remains the Canaries' record signing

At first the moves worked, and Norwich became a much more resolute defensive unit. Newsome settled into his role as captain and defensive lynchpin quickly, and from the start proved a crowd favourite. He also contributed a number of very important goals to the cause, including a bizarre finish after drifting past three defenders – the winner against Blackburn Rovers at Carrow Road. The build-up to the goal typified Newsome's qualities – his gritty determination to continue against the odds, and a comfort and skill with the ball on the deck that was surprising for a big central defender. This, combined with his aerial dominance, provided the Norwich defence with its star performer.

Throughout a difficult season, Newsome led by example, producing consistent performance after consistent performance. Rarely could you say he had a bad game, and with its key player absent, the defence looked exposed. The four-nil defeat at Anfield and the dismal two-nil reverse at QPR just two examples of a side missing its captain.

However, following a season dominated by Bryan Gunn's injury and a lack of regular goalscorers, Norwich lost their Premiership status with one game to go, after a controversial game at Leeds United. The picture of Newsome, kneeling on the Elland Road turf, head in hands, is one of the striking memories of Norwich City's relegation. He was all but universally voted the Norwich City player of the season, the emerging Darren Eadie his only realistic competitor for the award.

The skipper showed great loyalty in the close season and stayed to fight for Norwich's return to the Premiership, when he could have easily claimed a place in another Premiership side. Indeed, rumours had circulated during the previous season linking him with big-money moves to Blackburn Rovers, amongst others. As if to prove his worth and commitment to the club, he scored with two towering headers in Norwich's first game of the season at Luton Town. His quality on that day was something many teams in the First Division could not cope with.

Results declined following the departure of Martin O'Neill, and it became more apparent that Norwich were now in severe financial difficulty. This was highlighted when Newsome was sold in March 1996 to Sheffield Wednesday, the team he still supports, for a cut-price £1.6 million in one of Robert Chase's desperate attempts to stave off the debt collectors. The move turned out to be déjà vu for Newsome, as Wednesday were relegated at the end of the 1999–2000 season, and were to find themselves in similar financial difficulty a few years on. However, by then, at the age of twenty-nine, Newsome had seen his career cruelly cut short after a long and ultimately unsuccessful fight against injury.

In my mind Newsome remains the best centre-half I've seen play for Norwich since the fine displays of Messrs. Bruce and Watson in Norwich's Milk Cup and Division One Championship winning seasons. Without doubt one of the better pieces of transfer business done in recent times, it is just a pity that his contribution was not enjoyed for many more years at Carrow Road.

81

A stranger in the North Stand

Ipswich Town 1–2 Norwich City ⚽ Premier League ⚽ 19 September 1994

By Matt Hansell

Matt's first match at Carrow Road was a Division One draw against Charlton in the 1988/89 season when the Club finished fourth in the league.

Supporting Norwich over the last few seasons has been difficult at times, particularly away from home. My most uncomfortable experience was watching Norwich win away at Ipswich from the North Stand. For those who don't know Portman Road, the North Stand is where the hardcore Ipswich fans sit – a poor man's Barclay End, if you like. Not the sort of place to go if you are a Norwich fan.

I wasn't supposed to be going to the game, but an Ipswich-supporting friend had a spare ticket, and at the last moment I agreed to go. Now, call me naïve, call me stupid, but I didn't think it would be difficult. I had the opportunity to watch my team in the big derby at Portman Road for the first time, it didn't matter where I was sitting – the important thing was being there.

It hit me about two minutes after getting in the ground, when I heard the first anti-Norwich comment. Suddenly, I thought 'what am I doing here?' The feelings grew when the PA announcer said he wanted to hear from Norwich supporters, and proceeded to ask for the City fans in each stand to cheer. When he got to the North Stand he was met with absolute silence.

This could mean one of two things. Either all of us sensibly kept quiet, or I was the only one there. It was the second possibility that played on my mind. The PA announcer said 'no surprises there,' in a manner that implied 'who would be stupid enough to sit there anyway?' Still, if it was a test to uncover visiting supporters, I'd passed with flying colours.

And so the game began, in conditions so exceptionally wet that the lines on the pitch had been almost completely washed away. It was an unusual situation, but one we all found highly amusing. The game itself started very well for us, with stand-in striker Rob Newman giving us an early lead. 'How can a donkey like that score against us?' was the shout from behind. I believe I had a smug look on my face.

We then had the best opportunities to score again, until the first controversial decision of the night. Ian Marshall was brought down by John Newsome. No-one was sure if it was in the penalty area or not, including the referee, who took his time in awarding the penalty. It was one-all and I was the only person there who didn't find the situation with the pitch markings amusing any more.

The next controversial decision occurred early in the second half. Ian Crook

Bryan Gunn saves at the feet of Ian Marshall as City complete the first leg of the double over Town in 1994/95

was brought down in a similar position to the earlier penalty. This time there was even more uncertainty, and the referee signalled at first for a free kick. The Norwich players protested, and eventually the referee consulted the linesman. The whole ground was watching these two people talking in the corner of the pitch, then the referee turned around and pointed to the spot. 'He's given a penalty!' I shouted out excitedly, quickly adding 'I can't believe he's given the penalty!' and putting on my astonished face.

There was a chorus of boos as Carl Bradshaw placed the ball where the penalty spot was supposed to be. Bradshaw struck the ball as hard as he could, straight at their keeper, who pushed it out. The whole stand jumped into the air – I just sank. But the ball rebounded to Bradshaw, bouncing off his right shin and then his left thigh before landing in front of him. He poked it into the bottom corner of the net. Now the rest of the stand sank while I jumped into the air, remembering just in time to put my hands to my head as if disappointed! The Ipswich fans were too angry to care though, moaning that we only got the penalty because the officials couldn't see the lines. There can be a very fine line (pun intended) between amusement and anger. I was very amused.

We could have scored more – Crook hit the bar, Sheron hit the post and Goss was denied another wonder volley by a fine save. But there was something satisfying about beating Ipswich with a controversial refereeing decision.

As the final whistle went I looked to my left to see the jubilant Norwich supporters celebrating and smiling in our direction. How I wanted to take off my coat, show them my Norwich shirt and celebrate with them, let them know I was a Norwich fan. Sadly, that wasn't an option, and the only thing I could do was smile back as I left the ground.

I now realise that I wouldn't be able to do this again, at any ground. I don't know how I managed it at the time, all I know is that it was the most difficult match of my life, but also one of the greatest.

82

Tim has had a life-long love affair with the Canaries and recalls a 4–2 win over Leeds United in the great 1992/93 season as his best match.

Not the best travellers

Grimsby Town 0–1 Norwich City ⚽ FA Cup third round ⚽ 7 January 1995

By Tim Cook

The problem with writing about my most memorable City match is that I can't remember all that much about it. That may seem like a contradiction, but there is good reason for it, as I'll explain.

It was only the second away game I'd ever been to, the first being the infamous 1992 FA Cup semi-final against Sunderland. (It's just as well that we suffered the most appalling defeat in our history that day, otherwise this book would be full of accounts of our six-nil mauling of Liverpool in the final.)

Had I known that this chilly south Humberside Saturday would become so dear to my heart, I would have made more of an effort to remember it, or hired

Mike Sheron heads just over in the Canaries' Cup tie with Grimsby

a camcorder for the day. You see, ever since the Grimsby game, I've been to a total of twenty-two away matches, of which City have won precisely none. Twenty-two away matches without a win, each one of them combining to make that solitary victory at Blundell Park all the more special. If only I could remember more about it…

Let's see, there's the goal of course, a long-range effort from Ian Crook that utterly deceived the keeper. This being a match against Grimsby (one of those clubs, like Crystal Palace and Southampton, who seem to bring out the Herbie Hide in our heroes) there was a sending-off, and, er, that's about it really. Oh, and when Ian was setting himself up for the shot, I was screaming at him to pass the ball, which could explain why I've never got involved with coaching or management.

Norwich were drawn against Coventry City in the next round, so I decided to go to that game as well. It finished nil-nil, thanks mainly to Mike Sheron's ignorance of what to do in a one-on-one situation with the goalkeeper (here's a clue, Mike: you go around the keeper and score). However, we won the replay, and I set off with hope in my heart to the fifth-round tie at Everton.

Now, this game should have given a few clues to what I could expect in the six fruitless years that were to follow. Norwich were awful and lost five-nil, and were lucky not to lose by ten. The only highlight for us fans was signing 'Chase out!' and 'Deehan out!', a rarely heard example of simultaneous chairman/manager abuse. Mind you, it was a privilege to see one of the worst Norwich performances in recent memory, with Simon Tracy as bad in this match as Andy Marshall was good in the previous one. In fact, the only opposition that Simon has in this field is fellow stand-in Michael Watt, who flapped and panicked his way through a four-one trouncing at Sheffield Wednesday in 1999. Yes, I was there for that one as well.

I returned to Grimsby later in 1995 for a league match, but it ended in a two-two draw this time in a pulsating match that was far more memorable than the victory we'd achieved over them a few months previously. It had everything: end-to-end attacking, waves of pressure, dodgy refereeing, another red card and a last minute equaliser from Ade Akinbiyi. (Yes, I saw Ade score a goal! Perhaps I'm luckier than I think.)

However, from then on it's been lucky draws and drab defeat all the way. Lowlights of the twenty-two-game run include a three-one defeat at Barnet in the League Cup in 1997, which proved that on our day we could play as badly as anyone on the planet – apart from Ipswich, obviously. Another League Cup embarrassment came two years later, when we lost two-one at Cheltenham Town, who had been a non-league team just a few months before. This wasn't as bad as it sounds, as Norwich won three-two on aggregate, but my attempts to claim this as an away win were soundly dismissed by my travelling companions. Far more traumatic was the three-two league defeat at Crewe Alexandra in 1999, this being the famous occasion when we were two-nil up with eight minutes to go. How well I recall the words of wisdom spoken by a man sitting near me to his friend as we entered the eighty-second minute: 'We've won now, even we can't muck this one up.'

As I go on my travels, I feel like a one-hit-wonder pop star, making comeback after comeback, trying to repeat the glory of his one and only chart triumph. Will I ever double my away win total, and add to my mere memories of that day by the North Sea six years ago? My most memorable Norwich City match, and I can barely even remember it. I don't suppose anyone took any pictures at the game, did they, just to prove it actually happened?

1995

The old enemy crushed

Norwich City 3–0 Ipswich Town ⊙ Premier League ⊙ 20 March 1995

By Gary Cheeseman

Gary first saw Norwich City play against Sheffield United in the 1991/92 season. He describes here a memorable local derby which was to be his last match for two seasons.

The most memorable game I have watched Norwich play is – surprisingly – from Norwich's worst season in recent years. It is the three-nil home victory against Ipswich Town in the 1994/95 season. The game sticks in my memory not only because it was one of the most convincing victories over our East Anglian rivals in recent history, but also because it was the last game I would see for the next two seasons, as I was to emigrate to Australia. Through good luck I was able to be a ball boy for the game and witnessed the thrashing at first hand and at close range.

As I watched from the edge of the waterlogged pitch, the Canaries sealed the fate of Ipswich Town's season. The first half, though, showed little sign that it would explode into a great game; City seemed to struggle against a side who were already twelve points short of ensuring their survival. However, in the forty-fourth minute came the first hint of a vital Canary victory, the biggest of the season. The energetic young Darren Eadie made one of his sizzling runs at the defence which, as Canaries fans will know, would become a trademark of the Canaries' return to the First Division. John Wark lashed out at his speedy counterpart and was promptly sent off.

The dismissal proved to be the tonic the Canaries needed, and in the second half the game was turned on its head. With Mark Robins, Chris Sutton and Efan Ekoku now distant memories from UEFA Cup days, it often seemed that Ashley Ward was Norwich's only marksman. Now he was joined by two young strikers reaching their peaks. Jamie Cureton and Darren Eadie ripped apart their opponents' lagging defence with skill and raw pace. It took just ten minutes for them to affect the game, Cureton out-pacing his marker to find himself in a one-on-one with Craig Forrest after captain Jon Newsome had played the ball through

Ashley Ward fires home against Town

with pinpoint accuracy for him to run on to. Cureton took the ball round the Ipswich keeper and scored with ease. His goal was followed by a well-taken strike from Ashley Ward and some goal poaching-skill from the nineteen-year-old Eadie, finishing off a John Polston header after some scrappy goalkeeping.

With minutes to go, I watched from close range as Alex Mathie launched a header that looked certain to pull Ipswich back into the game, but it did nothing more than rattle the bar. The look of despair on Mathie's face and the chants of 'going down' from three sides of Carrow Road summed up a grand day for the Canaries, and one of horror for our East Anglian rivals.

After watching this demolition of our closest rivals I was able to leave for Australia in the knowledge that Norwich would be safe for another year. Having beaten Ipswich, we would have to get something pathetically impossible, like a single point out from a possible twenty-four, to get relegated. Which of course would never happen, I was thinking at the time. How could we be relegated after completing an impressive double over our neighbours and moving eight points clear of the relegation zone? Unfortunately though, as I would learn from a series of newspaper cuttings I read a month after the end of the season, that was exactly what happened.

So when I returned from my two years away I would have to watch First Division football. I could put up with that, but what shocked me most was to discover that the hero of the final match I saw at Carrow Road, Jamie Cureton, had been practically given away by the club.

84

The best team in the world

Grimsby Town 2–2 Norwich City ☙ First Division ☙ 23 September 1995

By Catherine Swallow

Blundell Park in Cleethorpes might not be the most auspicious of football grounds but for Catherine it will always remain the place where she first set eyes on the Canaries and her life changed forever.

My most memorable match also happened to be my first. It was at Blundell Park, Cleethorpes, when Norwich City took on Grimsby Town.

With two footy nuts for parents, I knew I would never really escape the torture of going to a match, however hard I tried. Sure enough, the day came when nothing I could do could prevent me from being dragged to nearby Grimsby Town to see the so-called 'best football team in the world.' 'Never mind', I thought to myself. 'I mean, how bad can it be? It'll be over soon and then I'll never have to go again.'

When we got to the ground, my mum bought me a drink and something to eat to keep me happy until kick-off, and we went to choose our seats. The team were warming up in front of us, but me being new to this football malarkey, I was oblivious, and turned round to see if the stadium was as big as the ones on TV. All of a sudden, a big white football came hurtling towards me, hit me in the

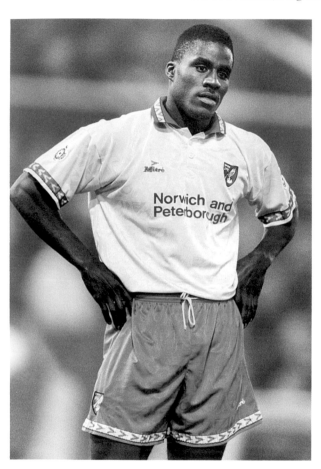

Ade Akinbiyi's late equaliser at Blundell Park sparked a pitch invasion from the visiting fans

stomach, and spilt orange squash all over my favourite white 'animals in danger' T-shirt. Robert Fleck found the whole thing very amusing and was on the floor in fits of laughter. I, on the other hand, did not see the funny side and turned to my mum and dad in tears, declaring, 'I'm not coming again.'

How wrong could I be? As soon as the match got underway, I was hooked. I loved the atmosphere of football, the singing, and jumping up and down like a loony when some bloke in a yellow shirt stuck the ball in the net.

That happened twice that afternoon. On-loan Fleck put the Canaries in front, the fans standing to sing his name, but two goals in two minutes, from Gary Childs and Nicky Southall, put Grimsby two-one up. Darren Eadie was sent off and the crowd began to shout rude things at the referee, which of course I didn't understand but joined in with anyway, much to my grandma's disgust when I told her about it later. The mood of the Norwich fans changed again when Ade Akinbiyi scored a late equaliser to make the score two-all. I couldn't have been looking, because the first I knew about it was when I was scared half to death by everybody jumping out of their seats shouting.

In the car on the way home I looked through the programme and picked out my favourite players – virtually the whole team, I think – and waved at a Norwich City bus carrying fans as we passed them on the road. I thought this football thing was great, and before I knew it I was going down to Carrow Road to watch the lads in yellow and green. Five seasons later I'm the biggest female footy nut alive, and try to drag my mum and dad to as many matches as possible!

85

South East Counties League Triumph

Norwich City Youth 4–0 Arsenal Youth ◐ South East Counties League ◐ 26 April 1997

By John Landamore

John has been a Canary fan since the '60s but more recently has become known as 'Mr Academy' following his great efforts in fundraising for the Canaries' Academy set up. John is currently the Chairman of FONCY (Friends of Norwich City Youth), as well as a regular contributor to the Club's matchday programme.

Joy for the young Canaries as they celebrate the South East Counties championship

With Chelsea snapping at their heels, City Youth needed to overcome Arsenal at Colney to claim the 1996–97 league title. Just seven days earlier they had faltered at Gillingham, losing by the only goal of the game, and so with one of the biggest crowds seen at Colney the stage was set for a showpiece end to the season.

Robert Green returned in goal after missing three games with a wrist injury, although for various reasons Keith Webb was without the services of Craig Bellamy, Adrian Forbes and Drew Broughton.

City could not find a way past the Gunners' defence in the first half, but with just five minutes gone in the second, Darren Kenton crossed for Trevor Walker to flick the ball on, allowing Chris Llewellyn the simplest of far-post headers. Che Wilson then went close for the Canaries before Adrian Coote scored the first of his two goals, this one a header from a corner coming after sixty-five minutes.

City certainly had their tails up. With fifteen minutes left Coote was dragged down in the box and referee Mr Sandell had no hesitation in pointing to the spot. Captain Joe Green converted the spot kick. It was left to Coote to complete

a memorable four-nil victory when he headed in his second deep in injury time. The lads were treated to a rousing reception, and there was even a lap of honour, much to the delight of the City faithful.

Gordon Bennett was youth development officer at that time, and he said at the time that we would never again see this quantity of quality players at any one time. Of the squad that season thirteen were offered professional contracts at Norwich, with nine of them going on to play for the first team. Four of them are still at Norwich and at the time of writing are members of Nigel Worthington's first-team squad.

86

Just to see a game

Hibernian 0–2 Norwich City ☾ Pre-season tour of Scotland ☾ 16 July 1997

By Richard Bland

Richard has been a Carrow Road regular since the '70s, but, as he describes here, cannot get enough of the Canaries follows the team on their pre-season tours.

Not satisfied with watching NCFC home and away during the season, in 1993 I embarked on a new venture: watching City play pre-season fixtures abroad.

Having done Sweden ('93), Holland and Belgium ('94), Northern Ireland ('95) and Eire ('96) and seeing all the games that were played on each visit, it came to 1997 and Scotland. This should be easy, shouldn't it?

Once the rumour had been confirmed that NCFC were to play Hibs, it was just a case of where – the match having been announced as being played 'behind closed doors'. Of course this statement made me all the more determined to attend. City could not confirm the match venue, so I emailed Hibs, but they didn't reply. I therefore set off around noon on the Tuesday for the 300-mile drive to Edinburgh.

The following morning it was straight down to Easter Road to find out where the game was being played. With no pitch markings and construction work being done on the perimeter track, it was evident that the game wouldn't be played there! Enquiries at the club offices were met with 'Sorry, it's being played behind closed doors, so we can't tell you where'.

Before setting off from England I had heard that the game in question might take place at Heriot-Watt University, so it was west across Edinburgh to the University, only to find the Ian St John Soccer School in place, including the little man himself. Extensive enquiries led to nothing but a list of six other possible venues but, as I was about to leave, I spotted a groundsman marking out a football pitch. I asked him if this was the pitch for NCFC, but no. I then asked him if he knew where Hibs trained, and he advised me to try a college in Crummond, north Edinburgh. On arrival I found Hibs' youth team in training. Once the session finished I asked the coach about our game and, at last, was given the venue as the pitch directly in front of me, with kick-off a mere two hours away.

I shared my information by 'phone with five other City fans who had travelled to Scotland, and they joined me and about a hundred others (mostly players and staff) on the touchline. Together we were able to witness Iwan Roberts score his first ever goal in NCFC colours.

The next match was at St Mirren – no problem – and then it was on to

Having joined the Canaries in the summer of 1997, Iwan Roberts scored his very first City goal against Hibernian

Greenock for City's final tour game. I arrived early, at 2pm for a 7.30pm kick-off, to find the ground open. I requested confirmation of the kick-off time, only to be told that the game was off. Having already inspected a perfect playing surface, I thought I was being wound up, until I was shown a local newspaper with the front page headline 'Vandals Wreck Morton Match'. 'Oh well', I thought, 'I'll just go home early'.

On inspecting the damage myself, I engaged in conversation with the Greenock Morton chairman, who gave me a conducted tour. During our time together a rumour spread (allegedly supplied by Robert Fleck on local radio) that NCFC had arranged a game with Dumbarton. The Chairman's secretary kindly phoned Dumbarton and confirmed that the match was on, with a 7.30pm kick-off. So it was off to Bog Head, Dumbarton, for the game which, despite reports, was not played 'behind closed doors'. Indeed, the match was totally 'open', in that admission was free to all.

Around a hundred people turned up, including a dozen or so Norfolk-based Canary fans who had heard about the match. Sadly, a few who had travelled up for the Greenock game did not learn of the rearrangement until the following day. For the record, just four Norfolk and Cambridgeshire City fans saw all three Scottish matches.

Even though I didn't go expecting too much from the football, it was one of the better pre-season tours for me.

87

Rubbish from the Binmen

Ipswich Town 0–1 Norwich City ○ First Division ○ 20 October 1998

By Graeme Davies

This is Graeme's second great moment in over a quarter of a century of following the Canaries.

As is well known, we have a major rivalry with a certain team from the Dark End of the A140 (no, not Cromer United), and derby victories are always extra special, particularly the away ones. As you would expect, our rivals have several nicknames, but one of the more printable ones is 'the Binmen'. This was derived from an episode of Lovejoy in which a refuse collector is delighted to discover an 'ITFC Wembley 1978' hat.

Whilst I don't claim to possess immense supernatural powers, I always know when we're going to defeat the Binmen. From the moment I enter the ground there I can tell just how happy I'm going to feel heading back up the road. I can simply sense it in the atmosphere. Over my many visits to the 'Stadium of Shame' I have often had this feeling, and to date I've never been wrong. What's more, I've gradually come to understand why it should be so.

Like virtually all local contests, the East Anglian derby is normally played in an atmosphere of unbridled hatred, and it is usually the team that wants to win the most on the day that prevails, regardless of current form. Drawn derbies are rare. Also, the attitude of supporters at derbies often spreads to the players on the pitch. I've come to appreciate that for us to win the game we have to hate them more than they hate us. It's because I can sense the mood in the visiting fans' area instantly that I can predict the probable outcome. If it's too relaxed, I know I need to worry. If it's tense and (frankly) downright nasty then I get a sudden surge of confidence. In more reflective moments I know that such behaviour is no real cause for pride. I've never been involved in hooliganism, nor do I wish to condone it, but when I'm at a derby I know the atmosphere has to be aggressive for us to win. This particular match was a case in point.

The Binmen probably helped us on that warm autumn night. The previous encounter had seen them put five past us without reply. Because of this, both team and fans were over-cocky, and seemed to assume that they just had to turn up to beat us. We, on the other hand, were interested in one thing: both the City team and their 1700-strong travelling support (that's all the tickets we were allowed) desperately wanted revenge, and it showed.

From the moment I arrived in the Portman Stand I could sense the desire. We kept up a non-stop barrage of noise all night long. Anything that moved in

Craig Bellamy heads home the winner at Portman Road in October 1998

the Churchman End was subjected to constant chants, as was every single one of their players as they emerged to warm up. Ours, on the other hand, were treated like heroes, and it was clear from their responses that they understood. We were truly united against the common enemy. All through this the home fans were either silent or occasionally reminded us of the previous scoreline. Bear in mind that all of this was before a ball was kicked!

The game started with City defending the goal at our end. Almost instantly David Johnson made a very late challenge right in front of us and got away without even being spoken to. After that passions rose even higher for City – team and fans. We simply tore into them, contesting every ball the way fans at derby games expect, and using the pace of Darren Eadie and Craig Bellamy to expose an ageing defence repeatedly. Ipswich offered very little threat in return.

Twice in the first half, Bellamy was put clean through to go one-on-one with their keeper Richard Wright, and twice he missed. But it didn't matter, and he knew it as well as we did. Midway through the half, Iwan Roberts connected with an Eadie cross and somehow missed an empty net from a yard out, but it still didn't matter. (His personal revenge for the jeers would come during our next visit.) This game was one-sided, both in terms of passion and chances, and it was only a matter of time. The whistle went for half-time, and the Binmen looked like the proverbial boxer saved by the bell.

The reprieve was only temporary. Although we allowed them more possession after the break, they were still not allowed to inflict any real damage – excluding yet another 'reckless' challenge by James Scrowcroft that resulted in Craig Fleming being stretchered off. Long shots and scrambled set pieces were all they had, and they became more and more desperate.

Then the moment was upon us. In the fifty-sixth minute, a series of short quick passes saw Darren Eadie running straight at the heart of their defence. A simple pass wide left to the overlapping Eric Fugelstadt and a first-time cross onto the head of Bellamy was all it took. The ball sailed past the outstretched arms of Wright and it was sheer pandemonium in the Portman Stand as Bellamy came running towards us, pointing cockily to the name on the back of his shirt. We cheered so loud and long that we needed a minute or two to recover our breath to start singing again. But, breath restored, sing we did – chorus after chorus of 'On the ball, City' and 'Oh Bellamy'.

So hopeless were our hosts that the possibility of an equaliser seemed remote, and our side's confidence grew. The only other real chance fell our way late on, when Roberts struck the post from thirty yards following a sliced Wright clearance. City wasted the final seconds in front of their jubilant supporters, and more scenes of pandemonium followed at the final whistle as the players came to acknowledge our delirious thanks. Sometimes it's just great to be locked in a ground after a game, especially when you can gloat over the demoralised Binmen as they leave.

The victory was mainly down to us having the greater commitment and desire. That made it a more typical derby success than our more tactically brilliant victory on our next visit to Ipswich.

88 Marc Libbra magic

Norwich City 2–0 Manchester City ○ **Division One** ○ **18 August 2001**

By Callum Butcher

Callum, at five years of age, is the youngest fan to contribute a great moment. Since first seeing Norwich City against Nottingham Forest in 2000, Callum has regularly made the trip to Carrow Road and beyond with mum Sharon, dad Robert and older brother Conor.

Manchester, they say, is the place where everyone supports City, while all those who follow United live in Lincoln or Kettering. That doesn't say much for one family who found home in a small Wigan suburb but kept their Norwich City season tickets all the same, and had to run the gauntlet of abuse from eager Blues on the opening day of the football season.

Arriving home at Manchester Piccadilly with Dad and elder brother in tow, we learnt that the day had just got worse. Norwich had been well and truly mauled four-nil at Millwall, while championship favourites Manchester City had beaten Gianluca Vialli's Watford.

And walking back to the car in our Canary tops we were reminded of how we

were going to be summarily thrashed next Saturday at Carrow Road.

It continued all week. Friends, neighbours and even the milkman got in on the act. He left a note saying if we beat them there'd be an extra pint in it for the Butcher family. My Dad left one back saying the lads had more bottle than he thought.

And on the Saturday itself, the procession towards Norwich consisted of sarcastic toots on the horn at every turn along the A17 and howls of derision as our usual café was taken over by Man City fans on their way to certain victory. My brother and me gave as good as we got though, and got an extra sausage from the café owner for our loyalty. 'There's only one City,' they sang. 'Norwich City,' we shouted.

Even my dad's boss gave us no chance. Quite why my old man ever agreed to work for a Man City fan was beyond the intelligence of a mere five-year-old like myself. But off to the north we toddled – well I did anyway – and we set up home in Wigan. Nice chap, my dad's boss, enjoys his football, and he invited us to join him in the Jarrold Top of the Terrace to enjoy the day's proceedings. But

Marc Libbra celebrates his quick-fire debut goal against Manchester City

my dad turned down the opportunity of dining in corporate splendour, preferring our usual pre-match venue of the Kings Arms instead.

And after our usual tipple of a pint or two of blackcurrant squash had been consumed with the anticipation of being bottom of the league at ten to five and the resultant agony of the journey home, we dragged ourselves off down the hill to the home of football itself. Whereupon we witnessed a rejuvenated Norwich City team take the game to Manchester City and restore our faith in all things yellow and green.

Carrow Road was a cacophony of noise – an atmosphere so different from previous seasons, almost intimidating. The first half came and went without any score, but both teams had chances. The second half was much the same, and with time passing away it looked like we would play the first two games of the season without scoring. I'd fallen asleep at the New Den, but there was no chance of that here as the game moved from end to end. Still, we looked like we were settling for a point.

But then, Iwan Roberts, my hero and star of City's last three seasons, made way for summer signing Marc Libbra, and no Canary follower will ever forget what happened next.

I can count to eleven seconds and I didn't need to get to twelve. The chants of 'Libbra, Libbra' were still ringing out around Carrow Road when Phil Mulryne chipped a free kick forward, Zema Abbey headed on and the Frenchman latched on to the ball. He turned one way, lifted the ball over Steve Howey, left him for dead as he turned the other way, and before the ball had touched the ground again he had smashed it into the back of the net.

Unbelievable, or as Libbra would say, incroyable. The stadium erupted as Libbra's name rang out once more and the players sprinted towards the centre circle to congratulate an instant City hero. The picture that would appear in the papers the following morning, with almost every player showing their delight, typified the team spirit that had arrived over the summer.

We were busy celebrating too, me on my dad's shoulders getting a closer look and begging him to turn round towards the pitch – he was looking at the glum look on his boss's face up behind the glass. That look got glummer a few minutes later when Mulryne again chipped into the danger zone and this time found Paul McVeigh, not much taller than me, but untouched by the non-existent Howey and ready to bury City's second past Weaver's despairing dive. The game was won.

The journey home was a memorable one, as our solitary Canary horn tooted at every opportunity when passing the silent Blues fans. Arriving back in Wigan, the neighbours who had waved their handkerchiefs at us earlier were strangely absent.

The local papers described the game in a different light. Norwich were dirty. The goals were hopeful punts. The referee missed too many blatant offences. Oh, and Steve Howey was described as a cultural defender. Well, where were you when Libbra scored Steve? Where were you? I was in the Barclay, with my dad and my brother, and I'll never forget it.

A Junior Canary writes

Sheffield Wednesday 0–5 Norwich City ◯ First Division ◯ 29 December 2001

By Conor Butcher

Like younger brother Callum, Conor has been following the Canaries around the country since he can remember.

Being a Junior Canary over the last few seasons hasn't been an awful lot of fun. We kids often sat there wondering why we'd ever bothered listening to Dad in the first place. It wasn't that I was even consulted about whether I wanted to go or not. I just got roped in. I didn't get a choice. Other kids got taken ten-pin bowling, sailing or even got the pleasure of just sitting in an armchair all day long doing nothing other than channel-hopping amongst the cartoon stations on Sky.

Instead of any of these, I had to accompany my dad on trips all over the country watching eleven blokes in green and yellow kicking a bag of wind about. And sometimes not very well either. I watched my Dad's waistline expand on a diet of real ale, steak and kidney pies and fish and chips on the way back. And I watched his blood pressure rise on account of City's poor performances too. At least that's why he said it was rising. Mum reckoned it was his diet.

Saturday was his day, he said. And by some stroke of bad luck it now appeared to be mine too. He even managed to get me to be a mascot once, at Huddersfield Town. They were bottom and hadn't won in five, or scored in four, or something like that. We lost two-nil.

Things had got so bad that in over fifty games I'd only ever seen the Canaries score three goals in a game once, and experienced triumph on their travels on a paltry two occasions. My little brother's record wasn't much cop either.

We'd discussed changing allegiance to watch a team nearer home. Manchester United sprang to mind, and we once went to watch Wigan too. We ended up

Gary Holt was voted Player of the Year in 2001–02 and scored arguably the Canaries' best goal of the season at Hillsborugh

thinking again. Dad said such behaviour was childish, and he expected better of a seven-year-old. But I only agreed to stay when he threatened to take my Playstation away.

And in any case, he said this was our year. 'Funny,' I thought. 'I'm sure he's said that before'. But this time round, he looked to have a point. After stunning wins against Manchester City, Wolves, Burnley and others, we were well placed for promotion as we approached the last game of the year at Hillsborough.

But I still had never seen us score four, and my run of away defeats was causing concern that I might be the jinx in the midst. But then something extraordinary happened. We won five-nil away from home. Yes it's true, Norwich City won five-nil away from home.

We were 1–0 up barely after I'd reached my seat. My hot dog bit the dust as everyone erupted around me. Darren Kenton notched the opener. Dad said he'd had a few beers the other night. He never runs like that when he's had one too many. If that's what happens when a player gets carpeted, as Dad puts it, whatever that means, why haven't they done it before?

Minutes later, we'd done it again. Some bloke called Nielsen who'd only been with us a few weeks decided that anything Kenton could do, he could do better, and the replacement hot dog went the same way as the net bulged once more.

By now, the rumblings of discontent amongst the Wednesday fans were turning into anger. And so it came to pass that half of them would decide shopping with the wife was a better option than watching their team succumb to the mighty Canaries. As the third lay nestling firmly in the back of the old onion bag, courtesy of Nielsen's boot once more, they all got up and left, returning home in time for the half-time round up. Still, the loyal sound of the junior Owls could be heard from their family enclosure. And I reflected that one's loyalty knows no bounds at such tender years.

And then, after three years during which I'd seen the Canaries score three just once, they bagged a fourth. Paul McVeigh, the only player in the City side smaller than me, popped up at the far post and smashed the ball home. Cue for a chorus of my favourite City song: 'We love you Paul McVeigh...' You know the rest.

At half time Dad was told off for hugging the nearest available human being

– a matchday steward with a charisma bypass. My hot dog was replaced once more and heartily consumed, and then we all settled down for another forty-five minutes of excitement.

That we only scored once in the second half was a trifle disappointing, but with the game already won it was hardly surprising. Still, it was the first time we'd won five-nil away from home since well before my Dad had even been thought of, let alone me.

Gary Holt bagged the fifth with the best goal I have ever seen. He collected the ball thirty yards out and launched a missile that flew into the top corner, nearly bursting the back of the net in the process. Last season I can't remember us scoring one from outside the area, but this guy's goals are never tap-ins. This was only his second goal for City, but both so far have been memorable, and so have his performances. Even more remarkable when you consider the poor bloke only has three lungs. Dad reckons Malky's got four.

The journey home was celebrated in typical Butcher family fashion with a trip to the boozer and a nosebag to boot. On the ball, City!

From boys to men

Barnsley 0–2 Norwich City ☾ Division One ☾ 13 April 2002

By Oliver Sweetman

Life-long City fan Oliver Sweetman recalls an afternoon in South Yorkshire that saw the Canaries take a giant step towards the 2001/2002 play-offs.

Attending away matches always conjures up a warm, smug sense of respectability. Like receiving your membership to the Gnasher club as a child or being able to talk about the latest Big Brother antics the next day at work, you feel the comfort of being one of the gang. To the casual observer, attending these matches indicates a die-hard loyalty. The hierarchy of fans starts with the bloke at work who went to Old Trafford once to the seasoned fan who has attended every match since the age of two, including pre-season friendlies, charity games and summer five-a-sides for the under-tens. By being able to converse about a recent away game, you gain instant acceptance as a 'real fan', worthy of a chat, a pint, or a nod of the head in passing.

It's even more comforting going to away games when you've allowed your allegiance to wane. At the time of this match I hadn't attended a game for more than three months. Everyone goes through periods when they can't fulfil all their commitments. Work, new love interest, lack of finances – there's a range of reasons for not going to games. Most are entirely reasonable, but none rid you of the low feeling in the back of your mind.

In my own case, the fact that I was living a hundred miles away, in east London, left me open to charges like 'fair-weather supporter', 'glory hunter' and 'plastic boy'. I was only a short step away from references to Manchester United. Something had to be done, and it had to be more extreme than attending an away match near home. I had to suffer for my disrespect like Fredo in The Godfather – to show my allegiance I had to travel to the furthest game I could. So I found myself driving to Barnsley on that Saturday up the M1.

The match had all the atmosphere that would reconfirm me as a paid-up Norwich City supporter. Norwich had started to suggest that they could end the instability of the past seven seasons in the First Division, quietly producing a consistent season. Now, coming to the final push, we had glided within striking distance of the play-offs. Our strength was our lack of credibility in the media. No big names meant no headlines, no pressure, and a will to prove everyone wrong. We crept up the table like a ninja in the dark, we walked over rice-paper without leaving a mark, we slid past candles without moving the flame, we were crouching tiger or hidden dragon, depending on your taste.

From your first experiences as a child, the buzz of approaching a football stadium never leaves you. The sheer size of the stands, the glimpse of the seats inside, the hustle of stewards and programme sellers, the smell of fast food, the colours of the two teams intermingling – the whole scene attracts attention. You know something important is going on and you are part of it. Wherever you are in the world it has the same excitement, something to stop and savour. It's life: more educational than any documentary or holiday guide, the occasion embodies the character of the town and its people. Barnsley Football Club was an amateur anthropologist's dream. The stadium was situated on the side of a hill among narrow, run-down streets. Behind its red and white plastic fixtures and fittings it maintained the appearance of a cow shed from a distant era. The Grimethorpe Colliery Brass Band played next to the club shop. Cheerful plump stewards with seventies-style moustaches pointed out the away stand, betwixt the coach car park and the pie stall.

The buzz of hopeful optimism had infected the away stand. Gone were the haggard end-of-season expressions. The crowd was in party mood. Fancy dress was seen among the green and yellow, inflatable toys bounced off the heads of the unsuspecting, faces were painted, flags flew and all the fans were kids again.

For me, matches like these, for all their importance, carnival atmosphere and emotional swings, just seem to fly by. I have to read the papers or watch the TV later on to learn the facts. The adrenaline makes the game seem surreal – time drifts away, events in the game are blurred and the crowd's interaction with the team is intensified. In such games I really believe that my constant encouragement to David Nielsen is helping him, my involuntary headers really are warning Mackay to clear the cross, and my constant chanting of 'we love you Paul McVeigh, despite your lack of height' will help the team to 'cross the ball so he'll score'. I remember the celebrations of the two scorers, the celebrations as the final whistle went, the undying belief in the road to Cardiff, players and supporters punching the air in unison as we cheered and cried for joy.

I can't remember the more mundane events of the game, but football isn't about detail when you're riding high. When you look back at matches you remember the buoyant optimism, the joy in the crowd, the unity between supporters and team and the hope that something fantastic was dawning. Barnsley versus Norwich was the start of the journey to Cardiff and a penalty shoot-out in front of 70,000 spectators and millions of television viewers. My memory of the day was reconfirming my love for Norwich City by travelling to see distant opposition and finding my team had grown up in my absence into contenders for the Premiership.

City fans show their delight as the final whistle blows at Oakwell

91

The manic six weeks

First Division play-offs ⚽ 2002

By Judy Trivett

This is Judy's second great moment from Norwich City Football Club history.

'We're going to run cheap travel to Barnsley.' I really didn't realise that Andy Cullen's statement was going to lead to the most manic six weeks since I started supporting City forty-two years ago. 'Great,' I thought. Just when it seemed we'd have a peaceful, stress-free end of season (well, as stress-free as looking after the Bus One regulars can be), it looked like I would be helping to organise twenty-odd buses. Of course I'd forgotten how football fans like a bargain, and the twenty buses were soon filled. Then we beat Palace and a smash-and-grab raid on Bradford City sparked wild celebrations amongst the travelling fans at Valley Parade. As we joyously departed Valley Parade to the usual musical accompaniment of Barty and the boys, we wondered – maybe, just maybe. City were back in the play-off hunt, and the number of buses rose to thirty-eight.

The following Saturday's draw with Grimsby seemed to put a bit of a dampener on play-off fever. As the Barnsley trip approached I had butterflies, hoping that it would be problem-free. In the event it ran like clockwork. My jitters disappeared as I watched the City fans arrive down the hill at Oakwell. The atmosphere was superb, with the fans all in carnival mood. The Bus One regulars (Bus Twelve that day) were in Bermuda shorts, my hair had changed from grey to a nice line in fluorescent yellow courtesy of Splat the Cat, and the bus was full of balloons and inflatables. I'm not sure what the inflatable dog was doing to the inflatable dragon, but that's another story. Other City fans in fancy dress, including Nora Batty outfits and cricket whites, were in great voice. But, best of all, the team responded and their play matched our mood. At half-time someone said Burnley were three down. Had I missed something? When did Burnley's goal difference get so close to ours? The butterflies returned – only these ones were destined to stay a month, had hobnailed boots, and were insomniacs.

The mood of the City fans at Barnsley seemed to have been brought home and rekindled for the Stockport match. The early sending-off, Mulryne's goal and whispered scorelines from other games all added to the tension. Then Malky sent the fans into raptures before the referee ended our regular season. Superstition prevented me putting on my radio to listen to those last few Burnley attacks. I just watched the faces of people with radios. I'm so glad I didn't know that Gazza was taking a free kick until after it happened. The massive roar

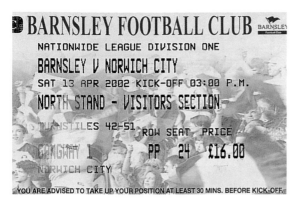

The fun started with a trip to Oakwell

signalled the end at Turf Moor. The scoreboard confirmed that we were on the road to Cardiff, and sparked the best end-of-season away supporters' bash so far.

This is the point where I seemed to lose touch with the outside world. Over the next three weeks the staff at Carrow Road worked wonders, dealing with two semi-finals and a final, planning, organising coaches, and shifting more merchandise than at Christmas. I spent a few hours helping stuff envelopes and assisting with coach organisation. In all honesty I probably wasn't needed, but I just couldn't stay away, and helping out was my excuse for being at Carrow Road.

At last came the Wolves match. The green and yellow cards held up as the teams came out were spectacular, and the atmosphere was easily the best at Carrow Road since Bayern Munich. I thought we played pretty well in the first half, despite the regular moaner (yes you David) near me in the River End saying that it was men against boys and we were out of our depth. The goals by Rivers and McVeigh early in the second half cranked up the volume even more. When has anyone heard the River End bellowing 'You're not singing any more' at Wolves fans? Then the crowning moment: Malky's soaring header. And no matter how much you try and tell yourself that there are still ninety minutes to go, you start dreaming of Cardiff.

Those butterflies were at it again as we left for Wolves – would the coaches fill up okay, had we picked everyone up, would the M6 be jammed as usual? Again the trip went well, but the butterflies were getting worse as we approached Molineux. What followed was probably the most intense game I have ever watched, in the most frantically hysterical atmosphere I have ever been in. High behind the goal, we sang from start to finish. No one sat down. I did collapse once or twice, but the nice young men behind me (Bus One regulars again) pulled me upright. I certainly can't remember the City fans ever singing so loudly, or for so long. I remember Clint having a chance, then Iwan should have scored, and – oh no – Wolves scored, with thirteen minutes to go. Now I know what people mean when they say time stood still. How can thirteen minutes plus five minutes' injury time feel like five hours? Ask the City fans who were there. Then the relief – we were at Cardiff. Cue manic celebrations. I haven't been hugged by that many young men in years… I could get used to it!

And so to Cardiff. Again, the week before was a crazy period of hunt the steward, organise the coach, make sure my Bus One regulars are with me for the final game as they were for the first, and just make sure you've got the tickets. Oh, and those butterflies were really back with a vengeance.

Just about everyone reading this will know all about Cardiff. From the start there was the non-stop cavalcade of City coaches and cars on the motorway, and the magnificent stadium. Then the colour, the noise, the atmosphere outside as well as inside the ground, Daydream Believer (well, the regulars sang the right words), the superb City performance, and the twelve glorious minutes when we were in the Premiership. At the end was the heartbreak of penalties.

So back to the real world. Did anything dramatic happen outside my cocoon during April and May 2002? I don't know. I haven't watched the whole final on video yet, but when I do I know it will bring back so many great memories of the six manic weeks and remind me why I support this club. Could we bear to do it again next year? Of course we could, but someone get me some butterfly killer…

92

The dream lives on

Norwich City 3–1 Wolverhampton Wanderers ☾ First Division play-off semi-final ☾ 28 April 2002

By Simon Thomas

He may be familiar to millions as a presenter on *Blue Peter*, but come Saturday Simon is happy to be another face in crowd at Canary matches. A supporter since the early '80s he regularly makes the trip up the A11 to watch his local team.

Until a few days ago I was writing this piece about a game at Carrow Road against Aston Villa in the 1992/93 season. That was until Sunday April 28 2002, a game that will long remain in the recollections of those lucky enough to be there, a game that brought back fond memories of those famous games against Bayern Munich and Inter Milan.

When Norwich lost at home to Birmingham City on March 15, I, like many others, feared that the dream of making the play-offs was over. But with a brilliant end to the season, and that dramatic afternoon against Stockport, we found ourselves in with a chance of returning to the Premiership after so many years away.

I drove up on the Sunday morning from London, and on the latter stages of the A11 I passed many cars with Wolves scarves flapping boldly out of the window. Little did they or I know that later that day it would be the Wolves players doing the flapping.

The look on the Wolves players'
faces tells it all – the Canaries are
going to Cardiff

Outside Carrow Road there was a carnival atmosphere, much like there had been for the game the week before – painted faces, green wigs, brass bands and nervous anticipation. As the ground began to fill, the expectation of many fans (at least myself and those around me) was that Norwich would win, and take a lead to Molineux for the away leg. As the teams came out, everyone raised their yellow and green cards and sang a rousing rendition of 'On the ball, City'. Carrow Road looked awesome and sounded fantastic.

Then the drama began. Norwich were playing with confidence and Wolves looked decidedly nervous – the disappointment of losing out to the Baggies the week before still very evident. However, when Dean Sturridge slotted home with Wolves' first real opening of the game, I looked around at the other Canaries in the Upper Barclay and wondered what was to come. The team having done little to suggest they were going to draw level prior to half-time, I nipped down early to grab a pie to calm the nerves before the half-time rush.

The second half was one of the best I've ever had the pleasure of watching at Carrow Road. With Norwich having restored parity thanks to a strike from

2002

Rivers, and Iwan Roberts warming up on the touchline, I turned to the guy next to me and commented on how good it would be to bring Iwan on with the score at two-one. Within seconds Easton had turned in a cross from the left, and the diminutive Paul McVeigh met it and looped in a brilliant header beyond the defeated Oakes. The ground erupted and my sister (sitting beside me) found herself being thrown about by her jubilant brother.

Iwan came on to the pulsating chant of 'Iwan, Iwan'. Norwich looked menacing. As I looked to the scoreboard at the other end, showing ninety minutes had elapsed, it looked like we would be taking a slim but crucial lead to Wolves for the Wednesday. But as Notman won a free kick and Easton crossed it in, the mighty Malky Mackay rose (as he had done against Stockport the week before) and buried the ball into the Wolves onion bag. I can't remember who I hugged at that point, but it was brilliant. As the furore died down a little, it was a joy to see a mass of dejected Wolverines walking away, offering only empty gestures to the Barclay faithful as they went.

As I write this our road to Cardiff awaits the second leg at Molineux. But whatever the outcome, that April day at Carrow Road was a day that reminded you why you love football so much, and made me very proud to call myself a Canary.

93

Memory Match

Wolverhampton Wanderers 1–0 Norwich City ⚽ Play-off semi-final, second leg ⚽ 1 May 2002

By Neil Doncaster

Neil, the Club's Chief Executive, has no doubt that the play-off semi-final second leg against Wolverhampton Wanderers is his favourite match.

As the end of season 2001/02 approached, and the deadline for submitting my 'memory match' drew nearer, I became ever more spoilt for choice. For everyone involved in the roller-coaster ride of Nigel Worthington's first full season as manager, the memorable matches came thick and fast!

Others will have their own poignant memories of that season's FA Cup draw against Chelsea; the sea of green and yellow that greeted the team in their victory away to Barnsley, relegating the home team; the scenes at Carrow Road after the Stockport home game, when our debut performance in the First Division play-off finals was confirmed; the barnstorming three-one win at home to Wolves in the first leg of the play-off semis; and the monumental final in Cardiff against Birmingham.

But for me, in terms of sheer nervous exhaustion, one game above all looms large in my memory – the play-off semi-final second leg away to Wolverhampton Wanderers. We went to Molineux defending a 3 – 1 lead. With a recent Football League rule change removing the advantage of away goals, we knew that Wolves needed to score at least 2 goals to take the match into extra time. But still we were not confident.

My wife Zoe and I travelled up by car. In our anxiety not to be late, we managed to arrive in Wolverhampton 2 hours before kick-off. Ambling around the awe-inspiring old gold coloured stadium, the desperate confidence of the Wolves faithful was almost tangible. The pungent stench of the many burger vans, the local paper imploring their team to "do it for Sir Jack", the booing of the

Robert Green punches clear
on the never to be forgotten
night at Molineux

Norwich team bus as it pulled up to the stadium, all contributing to the malaise that we felt approaching kick-off.

The subdued meeting with the Wolves Directors ahead of the game did little to calm our pre-match nerves. The polite discussion, assessing the enormity of the potential prize for one of the two teams, only adding to the tension. With ten minutes to go to kick-off, we could stand it no longer and purposefully strode out to our seats. The noise, the colour, the loud confidence of the gold-clad masses stopped us in our tracks as, awestruck, we took it all in.

With Club President Mr Watling seated on our right and Sandra Worthington, the manager's wife, in front of us, the game kicked-off to tumultuous applause and cheers from both sets of fans. Norwich, in their all red away-strip, lined up in a familiar four-four-two formation with Robert Green in goal, Craig Fleming and Malky Mackay at centre-back, Darren Kenton at right-back, Adam Drury at left-back, Mark Rivers, Phil Mulryne, Gary Holt and Clint Easton across the middle and Paul McVeigh and David Nielsen up front. Wolves meanwhile lined up virtually identically to the side that faced City at Carrow Road just a few days earlier; the only change being influential winger Mark Kennedy who, returning from injury, took Adam Proudlock's place on the substitutes bench.

City's first scare of the night came on sixteen minutes as Craig Fleming sliced a clearance and Robert Green saved well from Nathan Blake's close range header. The rest of the half was a mixture of City standing firm at the back and Wolves players being booked as the home crowd began to get frustrated.

In the second half City talisman Iwan Roberts replaced injured David Nielsen and Wolves risked putting winger Kennedy on for Newton.

With thirteen minutes to go and the Wolves fans beginning to quieten as their hopes of a glorious return to the Premiership faded, the unthinkable happened. Kevin Cooper received the ball about thiry-five yards out and hit an unstoppable drive past Robert Green in the City goal. Cue pandemonium. The stadium erupted as the confidence momentarily drained out of the Carrow Road faithful.

At that stage, most of the 27,418 packed into Molineux expected Wolves to go on, inspired by that one moment of brilliance. But it wasn't to be.

Still with thirteen minutes remaining the City defence stood firm. Into a nail-biting five minutes of injury-time, and with the manager's wife and I counting down the minutes, it was suddenly over. The hordes of abject Wolves' fans trudged out into the night as delirium kicked-off on the yellow and green terraces opposite. And so onto Cardiff, and one of the most famous days in the Club's proud 100-year history.

94

Play-off heaven

Norwich City 3–1 Wolverhampton Wanderers ☾ Play-off semi-final, first leg. Wolverhampton Wanderers 1–0 Norwich City ☾ Play-off semi- final, second leg

By Adam Aiken

A fan since the early '80s, Adam first saw Norwich play away against Queen Park Rangers. At his first home game Norwich City took on Everton.

I know, I know – this is a bit of a cheat. But when it was time to sit down and finally decide on my favourite ever City game, I found that I couldn't. It's not that I was unable to decide what the best occasion was – in fact, that part was fairly easy.

The European campaign was brilliant, and before that the 1992–93 season was unforgettable. But the 2001/02 play-off campaign was out of this world, despite the final outcome – partly because of the achievement of getting there against all the odds, but mainly because the misery we had all been subjected to during the preceding seven years or so made it all the sweeter. But my favourite single game of that three-match campaign? It wasn't the final, because ultimately that ended in disappointment. It was the semi-final. And here's where I found it hard, so this is the cheat bit – my favourite Canaries game was actually two games, the 180+ minutes against Wolves that got us to Cardiff.

For sheer atmosphere, excitement, tension, adrenaline and noise, the two legs of the tie could not have been bettered. And how City rose to the occasion!

But it wasn't always that way, was it? We Norwich fans have got used to glorious failures in recent years – Villa Park in 1989, Hillsborough in 1992, Manchester United at Carrow Road in 1993. How many thousands of us really thought we could do it against Wolves?

Going one-nil down at Carrow Road was hard on the team. It was against the run of play, I seem to remember, but it was also what I had been half-expecting. This team that I love – oh, how they like to get my spirits up and then quickly let me down!

And this was all the confirmation I needed. I know there will be people who will accuse me of having no faith in my team, but it was probably an in-built defence mechanism, a kind of cushion that I had already mentally prepared.

I hadn't given up – I was simply resigned to what I thought was going to happen next.

And I bet I wasn't the only one.

But I was proved wrong. And in such glorious style, too. At half-time, the faces in the bar and in the queue for the toilets were glum, with people standing around moaning to each other. They looked like I felt.

But then the second half started – and what a second half it was! Just 10 minutes after kicking off, City drew level through Mark Rivers, and his season of underachievement was suddenly forgotten. A draw will be fine – let's just not throw it all away again, and we might yet have a chance at Molineux.

And then came Paul McVeigh and his superb header. Unbelievably, we were in the lead, and those half-time gloomy faces seemed a million miles away now. We were in control now and we had actually come from a goal down to be winning, a rarity this season.

Now, Wolves fans are not quite as unpopular with City supporters as Ipswich or Manchester United fans are, but they're not far off, are they? And they were gutted. Well and truly gutted. They weren't singing, they looked miserable ... and they were losing. What more could we ask for? But still it kept coming, and Malky

Malky Mackay and Craig Fleming are all smiles after overcoming Wolves

Mackay's last-minute goal was surely more than anyone could have expected, and it sent 20,000 of us in the ground into yellow heaven.

So, a few days later, it was off to Wolverhampton, in the middle of the beautiful Black Country. (I know everywhere is supposed to have its plus points and its negative points, but the West Midlands...?) Anyway, we walked into what we expected – the most hostile atmosphere I have ever known, and that includes trips to Millwall's old ground and derby matches with our 'friends' down the road.

All credit to the Wolves fans, though – they certainly got behind their team and created deafening noise throughout the game. And can any follower of the Canaries remember a more nerve-wracking finale? OK, so we had turned the tie around in the first leg at Carrow Road, but this is Norwich we're talking about, and we all know that our heroes always crack under pressure eventually. Don't they?

Well, actually, they didn't. And despite an eternity of injury time being added on to the end after Wolves got themselves back in it through a fluke goal (OK, through a brilliant strike), the players in their unfamiliar red away strip remained so calm, so cool, so composed – and made it look easy. The final whistle went, and by the time the players had left the pitch after some amazing celebrations, I realised that the baying pack of Wolves fans had sneaked out, their vitriol by now aimed at their club instead of at us. Still, we kept our mouths shut as we walked the couple of miles back to the car. There were police officers with vicious-looking dogs everywhere, and a low-flying helicopter seemingly only feet above us with its powerful searchlight, but it still didn't feel particularly safe. Our City colours were hidden from view, and we tried not to walk too nervously, or look too happy with ourselves.

But inside, I was turning somersaults – we were going to Cardiff.

I'd known all along that we would do it.

The rest is history, and we gave it one hell of a try in the final.

Would I like to go through it all again?

Part of me thinks not, because it was so cruel. If we are going to go up at any time in the future, let's go straight up. If not, we might as well finish seventh.

But that's all said sitting in the comfort (boredom?) of the close season, and the other part of me knows that there is absolutely nothing that can beat the adrenaline and excitement of actually being in the play-offs. So, yes – if we have the misfortune of spending many future years out of the top flight, I would like to go through it all again.

95

The game that summed up a season

Birmingham City 1–1 Norwich City (aet; Birmingham won 4–2 on penalties) ☾ **First Division play-off final** ☾ **12 May 2002**

By Olly Cook

Olly has fulfilled what must be the ultimate dream of many football fans, working for the Club he supports. In the 11 years since he saw his first match at Carrow Road, Olly has witnessed many unique moments, but it was the thrilling spectacle of the 2002 play-off final that topped them all.

I found it very hard to select my most memorable match. There was Jeremy Goss' testimonial match against Genoa, the local derbies against Ipswich, as well as numerous Premiership matches against giants such as Manchester United and Liverpool. All were unique, but the play-off final is without a doubt my most memorable match as a Norwich City supporter. That's original, you may think, but many factors made that match particularly significant to me.

I claim to have been a Norwich fan all my life, but in truth I have only been a committed follower for a few years. My regular visits to what is now known as 'Fortress' Carrow Road started during the 1995/96 season – our first back in Division One – with my brother and my dad, who introduced me to Norwich City. My short-term memories as a supporter have been of frustration and regret that we never really made the most of our Premiership glory days.

I began working at Norwich City in 2000. My perspective and attitude as a City fan changed dramatically in the year that followed, and a lot happened at the club too. In fact, even the most optimistic fan could never have wished for such a turnaround, and I believe that what made the 2001/02 season so great was its spontaneity.

Going into the season, many thought we were odds-on favourites to make the drop. I have always thought of myself as an optimist, not half as much as my brother though. For years he has been adamant that we would make a strong push for a play-off place, if not the top two. This year he couldn't have been more right – I would have been happy with seventh place!

City's first home match of the season set the scene for a home record that was to be worthy of champions. With the odd exception, every home game was highly entertaining. It was the first time in many years that I could appreciate watching a team with a mix of youth and experience playing with pride and passion, spurred on by crowds that could have sold twice over. It really was hair-raising stuff. A vital ingredient of success, missing for so long, was back – consistency!

My chosen match is particularly significant to me because it symbolises City's whole season and my experiences of 2001/02. The highs and the lows that I had felt throughout the season were all brought together in that one game.

I'd never been to a final of any sort before, so I had no idea what to expect on May 12. When I arrived in Cardiff I realised my preconception of what it would be like had been totally inaccurate. Even looking back I cannot explain the feeling. The streets were filled with yellow and green, and I felt immense pride. This first impression set the scene for an eventful day that will never be forgotten. As I took my seat two hours before kick-off, the Millennium Stadium made an even greater impact on me.

I watched events unfold. At kick-off, with barely a seat in sight, the crowd was in full flow, and with the roof closed every song, every beat of the drum, seemed to echo endlessly. It was at around this time I realised that this was the biggest game I had ever seen, and probably the biggest game of the players' lives too.

The first half flashed by, with the adrenaline pumping, and the second half went the same way – very entertaining, but goalless. The match went into extra time, and I became anxious about the Russian roulette of penalties. These feelings were momentarily erased when Iwan Roberts' head met Alex Notman's cross. His effort seemed to be going in slow motion, but as soon as I saw the ripple in the net I let out an uncontrollable cry of joy while leaping around like a caged animal. Such a reaction is common at a football match, but how strange

The City players prepare
for extra time in Cardiff

it is. When else in life do you find yourself going from one extreme to another, and hugging a complete stranger who happens to be sat next to you?

Once I had managed to restrain myself I reverted to my emotional state and as fans do, I feared the worst. 'Just look at it this way, they have to score two to win now Olly,' said my brother reassuringly. Well that didn't reassure me at all, so fickle is football. I knew he was just as anxious as I was.

The most annoying thing about Birmingham's equaliser was not the fact that the game now looked likely to go to penalties – we would have as much chance to win as they did – but the quietness of our fans in contrast to the bellowing Brummies. And it did go to penalties – again, something I'd never experienced, nor particularly looked forward to.

Penalty-taking had not been our forte in the 2001/02 season, and it was agonising missing the second and third attempts. The players looked drained, as did the fans. It was a haunting experience seeing Birmingham's final penalty hit the back of the net. I sat down and took a deep breath. Although it had been a bonus getting to Cardiff at all, I felt the same as the weeping fans around me – 'if only'.

In hindsight, what a fabulous game – football in Norfolk had been re-ignited, and 2001/02 had sent a message to English football that we were back in business. That day at Cardiff showed everyone what sort of team we are, a footballing team with solid foundations, and one word is enough to sum up the day and the season we had. Pride.

96

Remember the pride

Birmingham City 1–1 Norwich City ☼ **(aet; Birmingham won 4–2 on penalties)** ☼ **First Division play-off final** ☼ **12 May 2002**

By Rob Butcher

Head of the Wigan-based Canary supporting dynasty, Rob Butcher has been following the team since 1977 when he first saw Norwich City triumph over Liverpool at Carrow Road.

Despite the heart breaking penalties, City fans had a wonderful day at the Millennium Stadium

'Don't cry, Daddy.' Those were the words of my five-year-old son as Norwich City's Premiership ambition died in the magnificent surroundings of the Millennium Stadium in Cardiff. And he was right. I shouldn't have cried. For my disappointment, and that of every other Canary fan bedecked in a wonderful display of yellow and green, was tinged with a huge sense of pride too.

This was the City side, after all, that had been put together on a budget, had lost its biggest summer signing in the first game of the season and its top striker for a huge part of the season, and whom many pundits were tipping for relegation back in August.

But there we were, in awe at the wonderful stadium with its closed roof and electric atmosphere – and in awe at the effort and commitment to the cause that had got us within one game of a return to the top flight.

But it wasn't to be and as the hope ebbed away with every spot kick, the tears began to well up. And then they flowed.

The fairy tale had begun back in March. Iwan Roberts was injured, we'd had a bad run and were six points off the play-offs. Other teams had made transfer deadline loan signings, but we'd made no such investment. The belief of even the most loyal City fan had been tested – most had simply written us off. We hadn't occupied a play-off position since early January.

But a terrific run of form with victories against Palace, Bradford, Barnsley and Stockport got us into the bun fight with one goal to spare. There were some amazing scenes at Carrow Road, and with nothing to lose we approached the two games against Wolves with the prospect of being without our figurehead, our top man, the toothless grinner himself, Iwan Roberts.

The prospect of Iwan edging his former club out of a play-off final berth and running out onto the turf at Cardiff to lead the Canaries to victory seemed forlorn. But edge Wolves out we did. And Iwan played his part, alongside some huge performances from every City player.

And off to Cardiff we went, with nothing to lose. Except the final, a £28 million windfall and Premiership football. No pressure lads, OK?

The procession of yellow and green along the M4 was tear-jerking in itself. For some it would have been their first taste of action for some time. Even my mum got her hands on a ticket, and she hasn't been for twenty years. Afterwards, she wanted a season ticket – but they'd sold out.

The atmosphere outside the stadium was remarkable – such a colourful scene. I didn't even bother with my normal pre-match pint. I just wanted to enjoy every moment, without beer goggles on for once. Inside was even better. The roof was closed, and balloons and flags were everywhere. Every pre-match song was belted out with gusto by the huge Canary following. Atomic Kitten. Fireworks.

And out came the teams to an unbelievable noise. Iwan hadn't started, but the game had, and for the first ten minutes we were pegged back. It didn't look good. But then we got ourselves back into the game and every man was huge. Nielsen and Easton went close with chances. Holt was magnificent in midfield, Malky a tower at the back. Rivers gave everything in running at their defence and at the other end Greeno made an unbelievable save just before the break.

McVeigh forced another one from Vaesen after half-time and chances went begging at each end. The Blues hit the woodwork but City were on top. Birmingham were pinned in their own half.

And then on came the man himself, with eight minutes left. Every story has a hero, and here he was, ready to finish off the final chapter in style. On came Alex Notman too, and with seconds left he crossed for Iwan but the ball was just out of reach and the game had ended without score.

Exhaustion on the pitch was matched in the stand but yet another rousing rendition of 'On the ball, City', the song that has accompanied City for so many years, rang out around the Millennium Stadium as we willed our heroes on for one last effort.

And forty seconds later after the restart, the players who had combined just before the final whistle did so again as Notman crossed for Roberts to head home. The fairy tale had come true. Barely back from injury, his former team beaten in the semi-final, he'd just scored the goal that would put City back into the Premiership at the home of Welsh football.

The celebrations were immense. Every player ran to congratulate the hero, who was on his knees in front of the City faithful. In the stands, tension died for a few moments and was replaced by joy.

But there were still twenty-nine minutes to go, and the lead didn't last. As soon as Geoff Horsfield had levelled past Greeno, something inside every City fan told us the fairy tale was over. It wasn't going to be a happy ending.

There were still chances before the game drifted away, at both ends, but none could be taken and a penalty shoot-out ensued. By which time the dream seemed over, especially when Birmingham got the luxury of taking the spot kicks in front of their own fans. And sure enough, the dream didn't come true. But one day it will.

For twelve wonderful footballing minutes we were there. Just remember that feeling. Remember the colour, the noise, the singing, the joy and the grief. Remember the players who gave every last drop of effort. Remember the manager and coach that got us there. Remember where we were just twelve months before and where the pundits expected us to be by the end of the season.

Above all, remember the tears but remember the pride at the same time. Remember it when you're considering staying at home when we play Brighton on a Tuesday night.

And remember the disappointment too. For when City return to the Premiership, it will make the pleasure that much greater.

On the ball, City.

97

Canaries on the charge

Birmingham City 1–1 Norwich City ☾ (aet; Birmingham won 4–2 on penalties) ☾ First Division play-off final ☾ 12 May 2002

By Charles Clarke

Charles, Labour MP for Norwich South, and his family have been Norwich City supporters since coming to live in the city when Charles won his constituency in the 1997 election. Now he is a regular in the Upper Barclay along with Norwich's other Canary-loving politician, Ian Gibson.

The best moment for any Canaries' fan in recent times must surely have been Iwan Roberts' goal at the beginning of extra time in the Millennium Stadium in Cardiff. It should have been the golden goal to put Norwich City Football Club into the Premiership – as it would have been in this year's World Cup Finals. Instead the players and all of us had to suffer the sad torment of a penalty shoot-out which brings random injustice after a fair and hard-fought game.

For my family the Cardiff game was the climax of a five-year infatuation with the Club. In 1997 I had been adopted as Labour's candidate for the forthcoming General Election. I did not have a close history with the City but we decided that if I won, the family would move here. We did win and so we moved, which – as every family that moves knows – can be a difficult time.

What made our move so much easier was Norwich City Football Club. We hadn't been big football-watchers in London, except on television, and we'd never supported any team particularly strongly – though I'd followed Arsenal quite a lot in their 1970–1 double season, which only went to prove that it was indeed then 'boring Arsenal'.

Charles Clarke recalls the play-off final as his best moment of watching City

But when we moved, we decided that we'd go and watch at Carrow Road regularly. I'd first gone with my children to watch the game against Crystal Palace in 1996. That game was a one-one draw, including a goal from Neil Adams and a 21–man brawl caused by the man who was to become a true embodiment of evil for Norfolk football, Kevin Muscat.

From that first game I discovered the very positive passion and excitement that motivates so many players and supporters, all conscious of the long and great history of the club.

And I also saw the tremendous sense of community that surrounds the team. It didn't take long to discover that almost everyone in the city was interested in the fate of the Canaries. As you left the ground, person after person would ask the score, who scored and how the game had been. Even friends of mine who had no interest at all in football wanted to know what had happened.

So since then, we've followed the ups and downs, week in, week out. We've seen brilliant players, some nationally renowned, others not so well known. We've seen the misfortune of injury destroying players' hopes on too many occasions. We've seen good results thrown away and wins plucked from nothing.

Of the Ipswich games, for me the most exciting was at Carrow Road when Robert Green made his debut so brilliantly, particularly for one so young.

Of the Cup games, the second half against Chelsea last season was just sustained brilliance, and we were very unlucky not to get the result. It was good at the reply at Stamford Bridge too, but it will be Zola's flicked goal there which will stick in the mind.

The individual goal which I remember best was Darren Eadie's, on return from yet another injury at the end of the season, against Crewe, when after a pass laid through by Adrian Coote he hit the ball from outside the area right into the top corner.

For me, during the time I've been watching, Eadie is the player who has most caught my imagination and symbolised everything attractive about Norwich City. I still miss the buzz which went around the ground every time he touched the ball.

So we now have our season tickets in the Upper Barclay, where we watch together with my fellow Norwich MP, Ian Gibson and from where we hope that the coming season really does lift us into the Premier league where we deserve to be.

That would be good for the Football Club, but it would be good for the whole community too. I remember going to a rather grand meeting at Holkham Hall with a variety of leaders of the Norfolk community. All the participants were asked to write down the thing which they thought would make the biggest difference to the Norfolk economy. The winner by a long way was that Norwich should get into the Premiership.

Let's hope we do this year. On the ball City!!

98

Standley has spent a phenomenal seven decades following the fortunes of Norwich City. In that time the ground has changed, along with the supporters and countless players and managers, but one thing remains constant, Standley's loyalty to the team.

Recollections of a supporter

By Standley Bushell

I caught my first sight of yellow and green when sneaking into the Nest around 1933 to see the last ten minutes or so of a reserve match after school on a Thursday.

Later, I was allowed to pay my sixpence to go to First XI matches at the front of the sunken terrace opposite the grandstand. I recall being in the 'chicken run' with my parents to watch the 1935 Hospital Cup game against Arsenal.

I attended the first match at Carrow Road – a four-three victory against West Ham. The first goal was scored by the popular Dougie Lochhead. I was present when George VI came to Carrow Road to watch part of the match against Millwall, after he had opened City Hall.

Then came the War. There were various matches with teams picked from servicemen in the area. On one such occasion I was very impressed by the safe hands of an unknown goalkeeper. It was Ken Nethercott, who would famously remain with City up to the cup run in 1959.

For some years I deserted football for hockey, but the interest remained, and I gradually settled on alternating umpiring hockey with watching City First XI home matches.

Having followed the cup run from the snow-covered victory over Manchester

Carrow Road was officially opened by Club President Russell Colman on 31 August 1935

United through to the first semi-final against Luton at White Hart Lane, the logical step was to become a season ticket holder, which I have been since 1960: first in the wooden stand, and since the rebuilding in the City Stand. For the last four seasons I have been joined by my wife.

I have lost count of the managers and players involved in that time. The club, the ground, and the many types of spectator have all changed too. There have been downs – re-election to the old Third Division South – and ups – participation in the old First Division.

We can enjoy memories, but hope springs eternal that we continue to enjoy our football, good and bad, and look forward to promotion to the Premiership in our lifetimes.

Aunt Erica, who says she attended her first match before records began, here offers not just one but 100 of the moments that have seen her through the highs and lows of so many years of supporting the Canaries.

My hundred best moments

By Erica Halfhold-Nelson

So you want to hear your Aunt Erica's hundred best moments? What type of book is this? Oh, I see.

As I told some BBC bod who shoved a microphone under my nose as we left the Olympic Stadium, 'of course I can't explain how it feels – you have to have lived it'. So here I offer only the bare threads of my life. Like…

1   Kissing the Lord Mayor for luck (he was planting trees on Riverside) before we beat Blackpool 5–1 on a sunny day when Division One loomed really close

2   The Old Trafford din suddenly turned off like a television as Ted MacDougall equalised late in the League Cup semi-final

3   Successfully aiming a cushion at Lol Morgan

4   Falling asleep in Finsbury Park after a couple of Mackesons to celebrate putting Arsenal out of the Cup at Highbury in 1954

5   Near-amnesia induced by two pints of 'Roger and Out' after losing the Hillsborough semi-final

6   Being third on the pitch after we beat Southend to get up to Division Two

7   Ian Culverhouse scoring

8   Being the first person to ask Howard Platt to play 'Down Town'

9   Beating Stoke six-nil and getting Stan Matthews' autograph on a Toffo wrapper

10   Orient

11   A last fond look at Wembley after losing to Spurs and thinking I'd probably never go back

12   Avoiding drowning at Chelsea as we won there to (we thought) stay up in 1984/85

13   Libbra's hat-trick at Fakenham and nineteen-second goal

14   Mark Halsey getting sent off at Newcastle on his debut

15   A nip of something warming during youth games at Trowse

16   That 1958/59 cup run thing

17   Being pushed in the plunge bath with Gerry Mannion

18   Arriving at one o'clock for our first game in the First Division and wondering where everyone was

19   Odsal

20   Taking a whole film of the scoreboard showing us one up in the Olympic Stadium

21   The exodus to York in 1974/75

22   Winning the Youth Cup at Goodison

23   Being north Norfolk 'Penny on the Ball' Agent of the Year for four years (until that ridiculous court order against me)

24   The train announcer singing 'On the ball, City' on the train home from Wembley

25   Borrowing the Barry Butler Trophy to display my irises at the Sheringham Townswomen's Guild Flower Show

26   Keelan making three saves at Turf Moor that were just not possible

27   Always beating the ban at Luton

28   A stand full of inflatable canaries at Upton Park

29   Letting Ron Stolworthy sell me a dozen rosettes as Christmas presents in the old Supporters' Club Shop in King Street

30   Winning the national six-a-sides

31   Simon Roy singing

32   Surviving the Den in 1974/75

33   Ron Davies heading the ball

34   Getting on the train at West Runton and finding the handful of regulars had multiplied into hundreds (though not by interbreeding of course) because we were going to Wembley

Aunt Erica

62	A slightly embarrassing close-up of me on the big screens at Carrow Road as Bellamy scored at Portman Road in '98
63	And O'Neill scoring against them
64	And Mendham
65	And Allcock
66	And Laurie Sheffield
67	And Anderson
68	And Bone
69	And Bertschin
70	And Cureton
71	And Eadie, accidentally spilling my soup over Jimmy Case's suit outside the Goldstone Ground
72	The Milk Cup Final celebrations
73	Peter Morris scoring against QPR to stop them winning the League (no, really, QPR!) in 1975/76
74	Lifting Eric Nattswortley's wife in the air and bouncing her up and down at Hillsborough as the result came through from Leicester and, miraculously, we were promoted in 1981/82
75	Hot Cross Bone Day
76	Fleck's goal at Millwall
77	Balancing between George Roberts' shoulders and the Bonds sign at the back of the River End for a cup match
78	Mel Machin's hat-trick at Forest
79	Listening to six grown men playing 'guess what colour car will be next over Carrow railway bridge' for four hours while we queued for tickets
80	Getting plastered by Tim Sheppard after cutting my thumb on the tea hut door at Kilkenny City and then getting plastered with him after the match
81	Justin's goal of the season
82	Flying to Oldham
83	Emerging grumpily from the ladies' facilities at Boothferry Park to interrupt a Match of the Week interview
84	Standing on the enormous terrace at The Valley
85	That disgraceful scoreboard incident
86	Polston's late winner against Villa leaving us top of the Premier League in late March
87	Paddon's hat-trick at Highbury

2002

It was only a hundred you wanted, wasn't it?

100

That Winning Feeling

By Delia Smith

The everyday story of football told in the far east (of England) is gathering such pace and momentum of late we can hardly contain ourselves. One quarter of the 2002/03 league season has whizzed by and (I'll say it very quickly) we're number three in the table, unbeaten away, have lost only once at home and have won no less than 18 league matches since last March!

'How lovely for you Delia', I can hear you saying. And yes it is, but – and I'm not quite sure how to explain this – all that ecstasy is partnered by new and unfamiliar agony.

I suppose it's that old cliché about life being tough at the top and all that. But what I've now come to understand is how very easy life seemed to be in the relative comfort-zone of mid-table mediocrity. For seven years, apart from a few brief, nail-biting encounters with the threat of relegation, the living was easy. The lack of any real expectation and learning to live with perpetual disappointment somehow doesn't seem to cost you anything.

Not so now! Life is lived at the very edge. I feel like the best man at a wedding: instead of 'unaccustomed as I am to public speaking…', it's 'unaccustomed as I am to winning…'. Every single match is like a play-off final. After basking in the glow of the latest win on Sunday, the build-up starts on Monday and when Saturday comes I'm reduced to quivering jelly.

I am trying to get a grip and be cool about it, but we still have another 36 games to play with 108 points up for grabs. How can I possibly stay cool? It's not even as if we're highly rated by the press and pundits. We have tremendous spirit, work really hard and play a good passing game! But even I, with my self-confessed lack of technical expertise, can understand that if goals get the results, then the one who gets the most is the better team on the day.

So while the butterflies in my stomach are on double time and my heart will be thumping in my chest on Saturday afternoon, I am filled with pride and hope and if, if we win life can't get any better.

TV super-cook, successful author, major shareholder at NCFC – since becoming a Director in 1996, Delia, undoubtedly the Club's most famous supporter, has worked tirelessly to raise the profile of Norwich City and ensure that time, money and effort are invested so that supporters now and in the future can continue to enjoy many great footballing memories.

All smiles – Delia is happy with the Canaries start to the 2002/03 season

Norwich City
Football Club